HACKING
LIFE AFTER
50

HACKING
LIFE AFTER

10 WAYS TO BEAT FATHER TIME AND LIVE A LONG, HEALTHY, **JOY-FILLED LIFE**

HACK
Learning
LIFE

JAMES ALAN STURTEVANT
& MARK BARNES

Hacking Life After 50
© 2023 by Times 10 Publications
Highland Heights, OH 44143 USA
Website: 10publications.com

All web links in this book are correct as of the publication date but may be inactive or otherwise modified since that time.

Name brands should not be considered endorsements by the authors and/or Times 10 Publications.

The authors are not licensed health care providers and represent that they have no expertise in diagnosing, examining, or treating medical conditions of any kind, or in determining the effect of any specific exercise or nutrition plan on a medical condition.

Cover and Interior Design by Steven Plummer
Editing by Jennifer Jas

Paperback ISBN: 978-1-956512-41-0
eBook ISBN: 978-1-956512-43-4
Hardcover ISBN: 978-1-956512-42-7

Library of Congress Cataloging-in-Publication Data is available for this title.

First Printing: September 2023

CONTENTS

From the Publisher

NEW FROM THE CREATOR OF THE GLOBALLY RENOWNED HACK LEARNING SERIES

Aᴮᴛᴇʀ ᴀʟᴍᴏsᴛ ᴀ decade of helping educators turn problems into solutions, Times 10 Publications applies the same simple-to-follow protocol to this new series to help all of us overcome life challenges. Hack Learning Life books center on what you already know and provide short-cuts to make life a little easier—who doesn't need this?

Based on the same practical six-part framework from the Hack Learning Series for educators, Hack Learning Life helps you unpack the problem, identify quick wins, make a long-term plan for success, and overcome the obstacles that may slow you down—all while providing stories from the authors or from people like you, doing the work and finding success.

REBRANDING THE HACKER

A hacker is someone who explores programmable systems and molds them into a different form, often a better one. Hackers are known as computer geeks—people who like to take applications and algorithms to places their designers never intended. Today, hackers are much more. They are people who explore many ideas both in and out of the technology world. They are tinkerers and fixers. They see solutions to problems that other people do not see.

Steve Jobs and Mark Zuckerberg might be considered technology's greatest hackers. No one taught them how to build an operating system or a social network, but they saw possibilities that others couldn't see. Hack Learning Life is a collection of books written by people who, like Jobs and Zuckerberg, see things through a different lens.

They are practitioners, researchers, coaches, nutritionists, professionals, and specialists. They live to solve problems whose solutions, in many cases, already exist but may need to be hacked. In other words, the problem needs to be turned upside down or viewed from another perspective. Its fix may appear unreasonable to those plagued by the issue. To the hacker, though, the solution is evident, and with a little hacking, it will be as clear and beautiful as a gracefully designed smartphone or a powerful social network.

INSIDE THE BOOKS

Hack Learning Life books are written by passionate people who are trained experts in their fields, or longtime practitioners, offering experiences that most readers do not have. Unlike your typical how-to books, Hack Learning Life books are light on research and statistics and heavy on practical advice from people who have experienced the problems about which they write. Each book in the series contains chapters, called Hacks, which are composed of these sections:

- **The Problem:** Something you are currently wrestling with that doesn't yet have a clear-cut solution.

- **The Hack:** A brief description of the author's prescribed solution.

- **What You Can Do Tomorrow:** Ways you can take the Hack, or strategy, and implement it right away. These are practical, do-now strategies that readers can use immediately.

- **Building Momentum:** A step-by-step system for turning the do-nows into long-term habits.

- **Removing Obstacles:** A list of possible hurdles you might encounter in your attempt to implement the Hack and how to overcome them.

- **The Hack in Action:** A snapshot of someone who uses this Hack in their space and how they do it.

OUR PROMISE

Every Hack Learning Life book provides insight, imagination, engaging prose, practical advice, and even a little humor. When you read a Hack Learning Life book, you'll have solutions you didn't have before, and when you put our Hacks into action, your daily life will improve.

THINGS TO KNOW BEFORE READING

*Aging is not lost youth but a new stage
of opportunity and strength.*
— BETTY FRIEDAN, AMERICAN ACTIVIST

WELCOME TO LIFE after fifty. This book was written for you by people like you, and we know you've got questions. We'll begin by answering a few that we've anticipated.

WHAT ARE THE AFTER-50S?

If you're over fifty, you're in the club. There are no initiation requirements, nor will we haze you in some archaic probationary trial. You're one of us merely by the fact that you're still breathing air and ready to experience this next phase in your journey—we call it life's Act II.

When we were kids, fifty seemed ancient. Now, to us at least, it seems young. Our fiftieth birthdays are far back in our rearview mirrors, but each of us remembers what a significant life event turning fifty was. It was an interesting combination of sobering reality and exhilaration. We remember thinking, *How on earth am I over fifty years old?* We're all in that club now, so let's make the best of it. In fact, let's thrive.

Half a century is a long time. You were born in a much different world, and this new phase of life comes with splendid potential. For most After-50s, the life responsibilities begin to fade. This is a long process for most, and the writing is on the wall. When we turned fifty, we still had kids at home and we were immersed in our careers, but changes were coming for both of our families, and those changes came rapidly. We're both now semi-retired and we've become empty nesters. We don't have as much income, but we don't spend as much. We've both dealt with the exhausting and heartbreaking phenomenon of the health decline of parents, but in general, our lives are less complicated and less intense than they used to be. We've navigated health concerns. If you have just turned the tender age of fifty, you may not yet recognize this stage of life that we just described, but you probably will soon.

According to the Centers for Disease Control and Prevention, the average American lifespan is seventy-six years. This means that on average, we live just twenty-six years after our fiftieth birthday. That's simply not enough time. And what's more, American lifespans shrunk in the early 2020s. While COVID was no doubt the primary variable responsible, other lifestyle factors like poor diets, sedentary habits, and mental health challenges have contributed to longevity stagnation, if not regression.

We've decided that we're not going to participate in, or contribute to, this regression. We instead plan the following:

- to far exceed the average lifespan
- to live the last phase of life with vibrancy and joy
- to leverage our freedom and our resources

Our hope is to thrive until an advanced age. Author and longevity expert Peter Attia helps people prepare for what he calls the marginal decade, or the last ten years of a person's life, as indicated by a decline in physical and cognitive health and a potential withdrawal from active life. Our idea of beating Father Time is to postpone the marginal decade as long as possible while enjoying every day of life's Act II.

The good news is that many After-50s are embracing this stage. Some are downright giddy with their newfound freedom. They are healthier, more active, and wealthier than their parents were at similar ages. We hope to help you craft a life scenario like this.

WHY SHOULD WE LISTEN TO YOU?

The short answer is that we are both After-50s. We're navigating this life stage with you. Our decades of experience teaching at the K–12 level inspired our investigation style. We taught students to hunt for the most reliable sources. In writing this book, we practiced what we preached. We don't suffer from impostor syndrome because we're not pretending to be anything but what we are—two older guys who are doing well in our lives and are willing to share just how we're doing it. So in this regard, we are primary sources—which, as you remember from your high school composition class, are always the most valuable. And just like we've done and promoted, you'll want to seek professional guidance before you attempt to mimic any of the ideas and activities we describe. We cite plenty of experts in various fields, like the aforementioned Peter Attia, but we don't attempt to play doctor, dietitian, exercise physiologist, or psychologist.

Something else that is important to understand about us is that we aren't conspiracy theorists; we trust what highly acclaimed sources have to say about longevity. When we curated resources, we gave more credence to information from a source like the Mayo Clinic versus a popular YouTube video where the creator had no medical degree. At the same time and moving forward, we embrace the advance of knowledge and we are both open-minded.

Longevity is a rapidly evolving field of study. Views on diet and exercise seem to go through regular intellectual convulsions. We recently read a fascinating book called *Good to Go* by sports journalist Christie Aschwanden. This book examines the research into athletic recovery. Aschwanden details findings that undermine many sacred cows, such as the value of static stretching; overhydrating; and the use of ice in the rest, ice, compression, and elevation sequence (RICE protocol). We realize that what an expert says today might change tomorrow in light of new evidence. We embrace this rational disposition to the evolution of knowledge. We think you should too.

There's plenty about life after the age of fifty that is depressing. We have many friends who get discouraged by the obstacles that life presents in its later stages. Neither of us is immune to these emotional setbacks. It's tough to look in the mirror and not recognize that face staring back at you. It's sad to feel hesitant about being active because you're worried about injury or physical limitations. It's jarring to glance at one of your limbs and realize that your skin is starting to resemble a dry, parched lake bed. It's especially hard to lose loved ones or lose your sense of place or worth. What is particularly depressing about the aging process is that it is relentless.

But guess what? We both are enjoying life's Act II, and this is perhaps the primary reason you should listen to us. We attribute our success to how we've approached, and will continue to approach, our After-50s journey. When it comes to chasing down solutions about how to thrive:

- We research.

- We consult.

- We experiment.

- We play.

- We reflect.

- We refine.

It should also be noted that we live in an amazing era of access. We certainly witnessed this revolution as it unfolded in our classrooms. When we were kids, the teacher was the gatekeeper of knowledge. The internet changed all of that. Artificial intelligence will amplify this phenomenon. The intellectual keys to the kingdom are available to anyone with a phone and Wi-Fi. We are living in a magical era that our younger selves could not have imagined. Please acknowledge and then exploit this wonderful opportunity.

Perhaps our greatest asset is our willingness to try things. When we encounter well-vetted ideas about how we can work out safely and efficiently, improve our sleep or diet, or expand our social network, we give them a try. We enjoy such forays into the unknown. This is why we listed "We play" in the prior bullet points. We're not afraid to try activities where we may feel or look silly. We're not afraid to try new skills where we have zero experience. Even if our attempts end in disappointment, we typically grow from them. Or, we'll take aspects of our experiments and use them as we move forward. Perhaps we can nurture a bold, pioneering After-50s attitude in you. Adopting such a disposition can be enlightening and fun, and it is a crucial part of the Momentum Mindset we mention throughout this book.

It is, though, important to note that our lives are far from perfect. We taught for decades. When you teach, your social interaction orbit is gargantuan. It's one of the best parts of the job. You may interact with over a hundred students daily, you have dear friends as colleagues, and you engage with parents and administrators in mostly positive ways. When you navigate through your community, you're a familiar face to many. When we migrated out of these roles, we both experienced a sense of mourning. We didn't regret ending our teaching careers, but we missed the people. Mark is now a successful entrepreneur, and Jim teaches part time at a local college. Neither of these roles has replicated the social interaction bonanza that was our K–12 teaching lives. In both of our cases, we now seek more social interaction, a greater sense of identity, and more feelings of contribution and belonging. We took these areas for granted when we taught, but now we would like to do some reclamation. Feelings of loneliness and isolation are common among many After-50s. We feel it at times, too.

In many ways, the challenge of writing this book was familiar to us. When you teach, you must understand a topic thoroughly before you can ever hope to present it to students. We particularly love the famous quote from writer Richard Bach, *You teach best what you most need to learn.*

We absolutely loved writing this book. We learned a heck of a lot in the process. We hope you will find what we have to say relevant, engaging, inspiring, and useful.

HOW DO I USE THIS BOOK?

We want you to consume the ten chapters, or Hacks, with an open mind. Each one provides a comprehensive approach to thriving after the age of fifty (Hack 10 is dedicated to the overall concept of thriving in life's Act II). If you embrace the goal of merely improving in the area each chapter explores, you will take a giant step forward. A primary way to accomplish this growth is to open your heart and mind before you dive into each Hack. Consider the potential of the ideas and strategies. Even if you don't embrace everything we share, you'll find nuggets that inspire you to at least investigate further. And speaking of investigation, that is what we want you to do. This is your life, your path, and your passion, and we'd love to act as docents on your After-50s journey.

WHY IS THE BOOK DIVIDED INTO FOUR PARTS?

To live a long, healthy, joy-filled life, we like to focus on four key areas. For the sake of clarity and easy consumption, we've broken the book's ten Hacks into these four parts:

1. Life, Act II

2. Physical Well-Being

3. Mental and Emotional Well-Being

4. Vitality, Impact, Community

We hope this will not only organize the book in a logical way but also make it easier for you to locate the ideas, stories, and strategies you want to revisit later.

WHAT'S WITH THE IMAGES AT THE BEGINNING OF EACH HACK?

We spent much of our lives delivering lessons to teenagers. One solid way to build anticipation in readers and listeners is to hook them prior to diving into a topic. One way to hook an audience is with a provocative image that asks people to speculate about its meaning. We're still teaching and can't help ourselves. We did this throughout, hoping each image will hook you enough that you'll want to keep reading to learn what the images symbolize.

WHOA! WHAT ABOUT THE TALKING HEADS?

"The Hack in Action sections are dedicated to examples of strategies in action. Our talking heads give us one more opportunity to share personal examples. My talking head identifies my anecdotes, and Jim's talking head identifies his."

"We also think the talking head images are pretty cool; we hope you enjoy this unique design."

CAN PEOPLE ACTUALLY BEAT FATHER TIME?

If your literal definition of this phrase is "living forever," we doubt you can defeat Father Time. For us, beating him is less about living forever than it is about living a long, healthy, joy-filled life many decades into life's Act II. Each day we do this, we feel we're winning this metaphorical battle, and we know you can too. Now, let the battle begin.

PART 1

LIFE, ACT II

Hack 1

CREATE PURPOSE

Life's Act II is an opportunity to experience life differently

Life is a series of natural and spontaneous changes. Don't resist them.
— LAO TZU, CHINESE PHILOSOPHER

THE PROBLEM: ACT II IS HERE, AND YOU'RE NOT SURE WHAT'S NEXT

YOU'RE IN THE After-50s club now. Your career is changing, it's winding down, or you may be retired. For many, this is like winning the lottery, only with retirement, you win time affluence instead of money. Lottery winners often splurge after securing their prize. We've heard many After-50s tell stories about initially catching up on all the shows they wanted to watch, reading books they had been too busy to read, and playing golf whenever the heck they felt like it. Often, the novelty of all this time affluence wears off. After a while, you might not feel good about watching TV at two in the afternoon, or your passion for a cherished hobby may diminish now that you can devote many more hours to it. What's more, some After-50s begin to feel like they're not contributing much. The world seems to have moved on and is functioning, and it barely notices them anymore. They can start to feel isolated—like observers and not participators. An old adage is still shared among successful After-50s: *You have to discover a reason to get up in the morning.* The objective of this Hack is to help you find that reason.

What's sad about life's Act II is that many of these realities fly in the face of expectations. We've heard working folks in their forties or younger regale us with their retirement dreams. They paint pictures of endless vacations and constant entertainment. Unless you're wealthy, you're going to spend a lot more of your After-50s life *not* on that dream vacation and, instead, wondering what's next.

Here are a handful of common sources of uncertainty. You may:

- have less income
- hold an unclear sense of identity
- interact with fewer people
- have less daily structure
- start to feel insignificant
- become pessimistic about where the world is heading

- be helping needy family members because now you have so much "free time"
- absolutely see signs of aging (no diversity of experience here)
- experience restlessness or boredom

This list could go on.

We know a few retirees who haven't handled their time affluence well. They remind us of unhinged college freshmen in their first semester. Some kids finally get out from under their parents' yoke, go to college, and then make terrible choices. Some "liberated" retirees make poor choices too. They overindulge. They spend way too much on items they don't need. They eat too much and pack on weight. They drink too much and pack on weight and develop dependencies. Jim joked with a post-working friend after a night of revelry at his house: *Wow, it would be pretty easy to become an alcoholic in retirement.* His friend responded with seriousness, *No kidding. You have to be careful.*

One of the hardest aspects of life's Act II is that you likely will have to cope with loss. This loss includes all the ideas we previously listed and also entails physical limitations, which will be more profound as the years pass. Plus, there is sure to be devastating losses of treasured friends and loved ones.

But there is good news. In fact, there's great news. Studies show that feelings of well-being improve significantly after age fifty. And this is not a temporary blip. Research points to increasing happiness as folks move through their senior years. What's ironic about this research is that it's counter-intuitive. When you see active kids and young people and the way they move so effortlessly, and then you think back to when you were that age and how you looked and felt in your body and how your future seemed limitless, it's easy to get jealous. No rational young person would trade places with an After-50. And yet, it's possible for you to be a lot more content than they are.

THE HACK: CREATE PURPOSE

You may have spent decades nursing, or managing a restaurant, or remodeling homes, but you're much more than these vocations. You did this work for a phase of your life. You're bigger than what you did for a living. Teaching is what we did, not who we are. Embracing this paradigm could be beneficial for After-50s, particularly those facing retirement.

You can have an incredibly fulfilling After-50s life, but no one will hand it to you. One person's fulfilling retirement of volunteering and doing yardwork would be another After-50s club member's hellscape. In order to create purpose in life's Act II—find that elusive reason to get up in the morning by answering these questions:

- What do you miss about being younger?
- What do you want your life to look like moving forward?
- What would you like to learn?

- What are your resources?

- What are some things that cause stress?

- Are you willing to take some chances?

Jim loves Margareta Magnusson's book *The Gentle Art of Swedish Death Cleaning: How to Free Yourself and Your Family from a Lifetime of Clutter.* While the title is a bit morbid, her message is positive and empowering. The book embraces the Scandinavian penchant for order, balance, frugality, and joy. The idea is that when you pass, you should not burden your children with having to clean up a house packed with unnecessary items. Magnusson's directive to purge unneeded items from your home can be applied to life's Act II both literally and metaphorically. Jim was convinced that his home was cluttered. You've probably accumulated too much stuff in your home too. Often, After-50s' excess baggage includes more than just the worn-out recliner that makes walking through the living room problematic. There's typically a lot of attachment that doesn't involve inanimate objects. Following Magnusson's advice, Jim decluttered not only his home but also his life.

"Now that I'm an empty nester, I've gotten even more serious about clearing clutter. I still acquire things, but when I do, I try to offset this act by purging something I no longer use. Every time I buy an article of clothing, like a shirt, I donate two shirts that I no longer wear. As a result, my closet is becoming a roomy and orderly space filled with items I really like."

The After-50s life is an intense experience. We both taught at the K–12 level for decades. When we navigated away from this phase of our lives, it was supremely difficult to not think of ourselves as teachers. Our identity was wrapped up in the honorable calling of being public educators. We both would've been well served to have cut our attachment to the identity of being a teacher prior to navigating to our current phase of life. It may be unnerving to think that you're no longer your profession, but a subtle and powerful change can occur with just a small semantic adjustment. When you reflect on your past life's Act I—refer to what you did, not what you were. Try talking about it in the following way: *For thirty-four years, I taught high school social studies,* as opposed to, *I was a high school social studies teacher for thirty-four years.* The former honors an accomplishment, while the latter sounds like you're going through an identity crisis.

Think of this Hack like many investigations you've conducted or conversations you've had. You explore an idea, and then organically, you're inspired to take a detour. You may find yourself in a place you never would've pursued independently. Start investigating ways that you can create purpose in your After-50s life, and who knows where you'll end up?

WHAT YOU CAN DO TOMORROW

This is a great roadmap for starting your process of creating purpose. Notice we say "starting." We both are still fully immersed in exploring and experimenting. We'll continue till our last breaths. Tackle these steps, and you'll be on a path of purpose too. This journey will be exciting.

- **List everything you miss about life prior to age fifty.** Make it as long as you like. You might include items about missing people—childhood friends or family members who have moved away or passed away, or colleagues from a prior job. Missing prior human interactions from life's Act I is a completely understandable reaction to an After-50s transition. So is missing physical aspects of your youth. The good news is that if you learn where your current deficiencies are, then you can act. We're confident this book will help. Hack 9 provides a roadmap for relationship-building in life's Act II. Part 2 of this book is devoted to helping you achieve then secure physical vitality. Understanding your needs will prime your receptiveness pump as you navigate the journey of reading this book.

- **Formulate After-50s rebuttals.** Take on this intellectual challenge. Formulate an After-50s rebuttal to every argument you created about missing your pre-fifties life. This is a challenge, and you may not be able to counter every example. We're confident, though, that you can come up with some zingers that'll put the younger you in its place. Check out our efforts:

What I miss about life before 50:	What I love about life after 50:
• Playing with my kids	• Playing with my grandkids
• Being youthful and energetic	• Having time to exercise
• Collaborating with colleagues to achieve goals	• Not having to deal with difficult people
• Routines	• Creating routines
• Big paychecks	• Lower expenses
• Helping clients	• Helping lots of people
• Excitement about the future	• WISDOM and PERSPECTIVE

The interesting realization for us when we read our side-by-side lists is that After-50s life looks pretty good. Just as important as knowing what you miss is taking stock of what you don't. We aim to help you build something new—something better.

- **Describe what some great After-50s days could look like.** Earlier, we promoted the idea that After-50s need to secure a reason to get up in the morning. If you wake up exhilarated, it's probably because you're looking forward to an event or activity. When you start stringing some exhilarating days together, you can end up with exhilarating weeks, then months, then years. The awesome news is that exhilarating days don't have to resemble one another. Act II offers you the opportunity for diverse experiences. Or, you might start a routine. At this juncture, compose a couple of brief narratives that describe the elements of a great day. It could include exercise, stimulating interactions, intellectual challenges, wonderful food, meaningful work, and a blissful afternoon nap. This exercise will be informative.

- **Identify what you'd like to learn.** In Part 4, we discuss growth; we do a joyous exploration of creative outlets. A huge part of your success in this area is your disposition:

  ‣ Are you willing to learn new things?

  ‣ Are you willing to be curious?

▸ Are you willing to be vulnerable?

Answering in the affirmative can facilitate massive growth. Many After-50s have the time affluence to pursue whatever interests them. If you want to learn a new language, take up martial arts, study philosophy, or become a wine connoisseur, now is your chance. All of this learning is great for your cognitive health, and you'll probably make new friends among your fellow seekers. But for now, all you need to do is make a list of areas that interest you and that you might like to learn about. Make the list as long as you can. Something on it will inspire a great opportunity.

- **Expose the detractors.** We all have areas in our lives that don't serve us and may, in fact, undermine us. Eliminating these stressors can be a major boost to our morale. The first step is to identify the culprits. You may have too much stuff cluttering your house. One unfortunate aspect of this stage of life is that you may also feel like a storage pod for your grown offspring's stuff. If clearing away excess stuff is an issue, put it on the list. You may be annoyed by the news or social media; if so, put it on the list. And finally, there may be individuals who, intentionally or not, undermine your outlook. Put them on the list too. Remember, this is for your consumption only.

- **Inventory your resources.** You've probably done a fair amount of networking in your day. Networking is a prime way to find a job and even land a significant other. Using networking to craft a more purposeful Act II is completely rational. Start a list of potential contacts tomorrow. This list can include friends, family, and associates. Also, list influential people from your past who may be willing to collaborate. You can also list local organizations that you may want to investigate, and please consider powerful national resources like the American Association of Retired Persons—geared toward helping folks like us. Include authors of books that have moved you or any podcast hosts that have inspired you. We want you to start this list by tomorrow, and like all successful networking efforts, your list will grow exponentially.

BUILDING MOMENTUM

In your quest to create a purposeful After-50s life, time may be your most valuable asset. Time affluence, though, can cause one to be indecisive—there's no pressure to make a decision, so it gets delayed. The strategies in the What You Can Do Tomorrow section are a great starting point. Hopefully, contemplating them was motivational. Now let's take this process even further.

Step 1: Leverage those rebuttals.

Earlier, we challenged you to form rebuttals to all the things you missed about being younger than fifty. Hopefully, these rebuttals will inspire you to love life's Act II, perhaps even more than Act I. Your rebuttals behave like springboards to After-50s fulfillment if you're willing to take bold initiatives. For instance, our second rebuttal—*Having time to exercise*—is an engraved invitation to a far superior existence. Building off the rebuttal inventory you created is a magnificent opportunity. This is far more than scoring debate points.

Step 2: Expand your investigation.

By now, we hope you've created a list of resources that can aid in your quest to create purpose in Act II. The more people who know about your plan, the more they can help. You may be reluctant to reach out to old colleagues, supervisors, classmates, or friends. This is understandable, but please try and take this step. It might be helpful even if it's a little embarrassing to ask for help. You could follow a script along these lines: *Hello! I'm X years old now and my life is different. I enjoy the freedom but miss interacting with people. I also want to feel like I'm contributing. You know me well. Do you have any ideas for me?* Then, be patient and wait for them to answer.

If you're greeted with "Let me think about it," that's fine, but please follow up with them. An important key in networking is to ask for another resource. *Do you know anyone else I should talk to?* Be willing to reach out to people you don't know. If you listen to a podcast interview with a fascinating guest who may be a resource, don't hesitate to send them an email and type, *I loved your interview about (insert topic).* Then, politely request a conversation. This may be a low-yield effort, but you never know. Thanks to technology, you aren't even out the cost of a postage stamp.

Step 3: Anticipate setbacks.

You may be surprised that we included this step, but entering life's Act II can shake your confidence. In many ways, it's like you're in your twenties again and searching for the right career. In your formative years, you probably explored some ideas and determined that they weren't for you. Also, you likely were told *No* at the conclusion of many coveted job interviews. It may have been a while since you put yourself out there so vulnerably, but it is worth it. Please understand that pursuing an idea and then becoming disillusioned with it is helpful. You can eliminate ideas. Jim has a friend who's an avid golfer. He loves it so much that he secured a job as a starter at a local course (like a traffic cop, this person makes sure people start their rounds when scheduled). He quickly learned that this is a highly stressful position. A lot of drama is involved with getting all these A-type personalities to wait their turn while they are out "relaxing" playing a round of golf. He laughs about it now, but he was disappointed at the time. He thought he would love that job, and he didn't. This setback came with a valuable lesson. Jim's friend learned that he does not want any type of role where he's dealing with upset customers. Welcome such powerful lessons.

Step 4: Clean house.

One amazing way to be more creative about your future is to declutter your present. We love the subtitle of Magnusson's book: *How to Free Yourself and Your Family from a Lifetime of Clutter.* We endorse the idea of you cleaning your house. If you're overwhelmed by all this speculating about your future, if you're not sure how to progress, start with this step. Emulate the ancient Chinese concept of feng shui—stimulating the flow of energy in your living space by creating a neat and orderly environment. Or, salute Admiral William McRaven, who wrote a fascinating book called *Make Your Bed: Little Things That Can Change Your Life … and Maybe the World.* One of his most powerful messages is that you need to get up and do something productive, and making your bed is a great choice. Once your surroundings are more orderly, you're in a better position to make an impact. We bet that you could make some strides in this area. If you have possessions that no longer serve you, give them to someone who needs them. Or, if these possessions wouldn't serve anyone, gather the gumption and throw them away. We believe strongly that creating a neat and orderly living space will prime your creative pump and aid in your quest to find your Act II purpose.

Step 5: Be open.

Who knows where this investigation may take you. If you've yet to retire, you may move to a new role or another company. You may find yourself working a part-time job. You may find yourself volunteering for a cause you're passionate about.

"I left teaching at age fifty to pursue writing. Unhappy with the publishing world, I began researching how to publish a book I was writing. Soon, I believed I could launch my own publishing company. Being open to something previously foreign to me led to an amazing second career in my Act II."

Through your networking, you may be presented with an idea or an opportunity that you never would've considered before. This open-minded search for joy and fulfillment might help you hone your purpose.

REMOVING OBSTACLES

Your Act II is a big deal. Whether you love it or you struggle with being part of the After-50s club, you live in a new world. Adaptation will happen whether you seek it or not. People who thrive in Act II are willing to evolve. But change isn't easy—particularly for more seasoned people. Here are common momentum blockers and their solutions.

I can't come up with rebuttals to my "what I miss about being younger than fifty" list. This doesn't surprise us. This was a stiff challenge, and it's tough to come up with responses when we put you on the spot. Perhaps copy down your list and post it on your fridge. Keep considering it every time you open the door. Maybe some rebuttals just need time to marinate before they make their dramatic appearance. Plus, you may have a rebuttal that hasn't come to mind. Mark, for example, missed hard workouts at the gym in his before-fifty years. Once he learned how to adapt his workout to his After-50s body, his rebuttal became, "I love exercising in fun new ways."

What if I find nothing that interests me? We deal with this fear frequently. We are people of action, and we want answers. It's frustrating when they don't come when summoned. Our best advice is to be patient. Believe that opportunities will present themselves. And then, just like Jim's friend experienced at the golf course, you may be completely disappointed. But searches are ultimately numbers games. The more open-minded you are, the more you explore and learn, and the better chance that you'll find an activity that gives you great purpose and makes you eager to get out of bed. (See Mark's talking head comment about this concept.)

I'm struggling with motivation. This can be an issue for many After-50s. They simply don't have the juice they once had. These feelings of attachment to the younger you can be quite powerful. It's completely natural, but please remember the research we cited earlier about the well-being and contentment of older people. You're probably happier than you realize, and you were probably less happy during Act I than you remember now. Also, we bet you're a far more together and wiser person than you were when you were in your thirties. Make certain to take stock of that. And if you need a shot of adrenaline, hop on the declutter train that we mentioned in the last section. Creating an orderly and nurturing space, built for exploration and open-mindedness, should give you a boost.

I wouldn't be comfortable asking for help. This is a tough one, for sure. Most people don't want to bother others. They don't want to be vulnerable. They don't want to announce publicly that they are struggling with this supposed blissful time. We understand, but the price of silence is too high. Do what needs to be done and reach out. Our experience shows that when you're vulnerable, people want to help.

I'm too rigid. If you're worried about becoming too inflexible as you age, watch a few videos on the internet showing irate people berating others for some innocuous behavior (you've probably seen dozens), and do everything in your power to behave differently. Change is hard, but change is natural. The world constantly evolves, and you trying to make it stationary or turn back the clock is impossible. Your life changes after fifty. Embrace this change.

THE HACK IN ACTION

Creating purpose in your After-50s life will involve trial and error. When it comes to trial, you need to gather the chutzpah to step out of your comfort zone and try things. Remember, now you have time to go on these excursions. When it comes to errors, don't be afraid to be unsatisfied many times. What's important is to learn from these experiences. Such analysis can lead to more refined future attempts.

Jim's story …

I live in suburban Columbus, Ohio. Columbus, which is situated deep in the heart of flyover country, is a vibrant place. One of our most important attributes is our diversity. Not only have we attracted immigrants, but we're also home to many refugees.

I retired from K–12 teaching in my late fifties. I've gone through a lot of trial and error. The summer after my exit, I decided to volunteer at a local organization helping refugees pass the American Citizenship Test. This was a challenging gig. I had a class of around fifteen adults of all ages. The language barrier between my students and me was imposing.

Still, I felt good about what I did. I volunteered long enough to see many of my students become American citizens.

Interestingly enough, I only taught this class for one summer. After that summer, I did a cost-benefit analysis of this endeavor (similar to the lists we discussed earlier). Here are my results:

What I liked:

- I was helping people. I loved my students. It was awesome when a student became a US citizen.

- It satisfied my need for social interaction.

- I was forced to do creative problem-solving because the school had limited resources and, of course, because I had to navigate significant language barriers.

- I was able to leverage my expertise.

What I didn't like:

- It was a lot of work for no pay.

- I had to drive thirty miles round trip to the school.

- I was bound to a schedule.

- It required time outside of class for lesson planning.

At the conclusion of this evaluation, I decided not to return to the school. I felt some remorse because I was effective, and there were, and are, plenty of students who need help. Also, I respect the organization and its mission. The school doesn't have many resources. There are few paid positions, and I wasn't angling for a full-time teaching gig anyway.

I decided this activity was not the right fit for me. What I learned is that if I volunteer in the future, I need to find an opportunity where I can help people and be intellectually and socially stimulated. I neither want to drive a long distance to do it, nor devote time to it when I'm not there. These were wonderful learnings, and they became clear through evaluating this experience.

I learned a lot about myself and about being a retired person in my brief stint teaching citizenship. And, I helped some nice people become Americans.

As previously mentioned, the great news is that research proves After-50s are, by and large, happier than younger global citizens. We don't look as good and our joints don't operate as freely, but we're happier. It's important to recognize and acknowledge the reasons behind these feelings of well-being and build on the foundations. This practice will ultimately lead to your purpose.

EMBRACE MOMENTUM

We have plenty to look forward to

*You are never too old to set another
goal or to dream a new dream.*
— C.S. LEWIS, AUTHOR AND SCHOLAR

THE PROBLEM: AFTER-50S SOMETIMES BELIEVE THEIR BEST DAYS ARE BEHIND THEM

IF YOU'RE AN After-50, you probably have more yesterdays than tomorrows. Some of us indeed may grow to be centenarians, but most of us won't. And if you are sixty or seventy, you are well past the halfway point. We all have a shelf life. It's rational to observe this reality and get depressed.

And it's not just the ticking clock and the accelerating calendar that bring us down—it's also the quality of our existence. We've all declined physically and perhaps even cognitively. Frankly, it's sad to see media stories featuring photos of older celebrities who are lauded for how well they've aged. A headline will read, *So and so is still turning heads at sixty!* The highly selective and perhaps enhanced snapshot that inspired this headline captures a brief moment in time. The reality represented by that image has already receded into the space-time continuum. This attractive celebrity will not look as good five years from now, and they will have to resort to more extreme measures to try to delay the inevitable.

It's often noted that attractive and popular people suffer aging more than we obscure folks. The adoration tends to dry up as their looks decline. Neither of us has ever been asked to pose for a photo shoot to make provocative posters for our legions of fans to hang on their walls. Maybe that's a blessing. Perhaps because of our lack of notoriety, we've coped with aging better. So if you've ever been a bit envious of your favorite hot movie star, consider that maybe at this stage of life, the tables have turned and they would trade places with you. But all of us, regardless of our popularity or good looks, miss our younger selves.

More profound than vanity is loneliness. Life after fifty can be isolating. You may be recently divorced or widowed. You may be single and have been so your whole life. Your parents may have passed or are in poor health. You may have recently had to euthanize your ancient and loyal dog whom you loved dearly. Your kids may have grown more independent—which is great except that you feel less needed. You've retired, or you're close to retiring. This means that everyone who you interacted with daily fades into memory. Most After-50s look forward to retirement, but it may come with unpleasant and unanticipated realities about a loss of identity and feelings of isolation.

It's easy to complain that your best days are behind you. Remember, negative thinking can be self-fulfilling. If you have children, you've probably admonished them about being too negative. Perhaps when they whined too much, lost in some adolescent drama, you scolded, *Enough of this negativity. It's defeating, and you're making yourself and everyone around you miserable.* That was great advice you gave then, and we're going to give you similar advice now. We hope to inspire you to recognize and then leverage the outstanding potential that life in this less-burdened phase has to offer. This Hack will set the stage for you to make great changes that will directly benefit you.

And finally, we need to mention other potential readers whose lives have always been largely unsatisfactory. They are not nostalgic about what was because their past life wasn't positive. If you fall into this category, you have the greatest opportunity for growth.

THE HACK: EMBRACE THE MOMENTUM MINDSET

When we looked up definitions of momentum, we often found the word *movement*. We also noticed that these definitions of momentum, if not explicitly stated, also implied forward movement or growth. Regarding definitions of mindset, we love this phrase we uncovered: *an established set of attitudes*. Our definition of the Momentum Mindset is as follows: "An established set of attitudes that are devoted to growth." This attitude will be the fuel that propels you through the remaining Hacks in this book. The key ingredients of this Momentum Mindset are a bold sense of curiosity, a yearning for adventure, a willingness to try and fail and then learn and adapt, and a keen desire to have more fun and more joy in your life.

You will also need to cut yourself some slack. Many of the ideas we promote may seem exotic compared to your past half-century of existence. Other ideas may seem like common sense and easy to at least grasp. Remember, though, just because an idea makes sense and you have every intention of implementing it—change is still hard, particularly for seasoned people with lots of miles on their odometers. We can all be pretty set in our ways. Please be patient and, just as important, evaluate your efforts objectively and acknowledge progress when it's present.

This idea of progress recognition brings to mind the important concept of incrementalism. This is a wonderful word that simply refers to gradual change. You may have ambitious social and fitness goals. We certainly applaud you if you do. Remember, though, none of us is training for the Olympic Games. Most of us have time affluence, so you can take your sweet time in realizing your goals, but you must be cognizant of all the growth you have achieved along the way.

If you stay open-minded and adapt the ideas in this

book to your lifestyle, we believe you will be a more vibrant person by the time you get to the last page. And it's totally natural if you have setbacks, alter your goals, or come up with replacement goals on the journey. When this occurs, look back to where you were when you started. This is how the Momentum Mindset will be served by observation and evaluation through the lens of incrementalism.

We strongly believe that After-50s should pursue activities that are enjoyable and that add to your life. You've lived, you've loved, and you've toiled for a long time. Others are probably cheering for you. You've celebrated with children, spouses, and bosses when they've achieved. Truth be told, they may not have achieved without your help. Now, it's your turn. Embrace this mindset, and let's have some fun.

WHAT YOU CAN DO TOMORROW

Embracing the Momentum Mindset might be a different experience after age fifty. When you were a young pup, you may have wanted to find a fulfilling career and do meaningful work you love, find the perfect spouse, and strive to be the fittest among your peers. Even if you didn't have such lofty goals, you probably had achievement intentions. Many of these goals relied on outward recognition from others—*Hey, you accomplished something great!* We don't mean to denigrate such ambitions. You may still have them. You want to look good, find love, and land more wealth, and you're thrilled when others notice such achievements. These longings don't migrate after fifty, and we applaud them, but we suggest that you adjust your focus. Apply your Momentum Mindset not for the approval of others but in pursuit of personal gratification.

"When I left full-time teaching, I decided I would read more, so I challenged myself to finish fifty books a year. This goal was just for me. I don't even talk about it with others. I love reading, and when I hit the goal, I feel better about myself. One key, though, is writing down the goal and keeping a list of to-read books."

Strive for goals that feel good—both literally and figuratively. Some of our ideas may prompt friends or relatives to ask, *Why are you doing such a thing at your age?* First, we want you to migrate away from always needing the approval of others. Don't worry if your peers think that going back to college at your age is silly. And second, such a statement may be inspired by a bit of envy. We suggest that you respond to any such query with, *I do this because it feels like the right thing for me right now.*

You may struggle with the following strategies. We'll revisit each one in later sections. But for the next twenty-four hours, contemplate these and write down your reactions. For many, this simple act is a great way to fuel your Momentum Mindset.

- **Inventory your limitations.** We aren't pollyannas. Once you pass fifty, new limitations emerge and old limitations are more imposing. We're not asking you to do the impossible or set overly ambitious goals. Neither of us will be fitness models, compete in the Olympics, or win the Nobel Peace Prize. We do embrace the Momentum Mindset, though. It's about becoming better versions of ourselves. It's positive and optimistic. But if you have physical limitations (as most do), or financial limitations, or social or familial obligations, or time obligations because you're still working, please make note of them. Understanding your After-50s limitations helps fuel your Momentum Mindset. Consider jotting down these limitations on paper. Then, reflect on them, as they can help inform your goals. We'll ask you to list those too.

- **Set a health and fitness goal.** We sometimes reference being an After-50 as having a lot of miles on our odometers, which clearly creates an analogy of the body as a vehicle. It's an apt comparison because our bodies, unfortunately, are also depreciating assets. Unlike a car, there's no option to trade in your body for a newer model. So if we're stuck with our bodies, let's fix them up and make better versions of whatever genetic cocktail we've been assigned. If you could improve aspects of your physical well-being, what would they be? That's your assignment for tomorrow (or today, if you're eager to get started). Creating clear objectives is a great first step in the Momentum Mindset. Part 2 of this book will help you realize your goals and, in the process, perhaps inspire more ambitious and diverse goals. Remember, writing these down will come in handy later when we ask you to revisit them.

- **Set an emotional well-being goal.** Getting healthier, feeling good, and looking vibrant are all great ambitions, but you can realize your goal of looking and feeling younger and still be fundamentally unhappy. You may feel lonely, unloved, isolated, unneeded, dependent, out-of-touch, or any of the myriad of human deficit emotions. If you could improve aspects of your emotional well-being, what would they be? That's your assignment that you can do right away. Part 3 will empower you to help realize your objectives in this realm. Remember, we will ask you to revisit this list later.

- **Set a community engagement goal.** Gaining momentum regarding your physical and emotional well-being is a noble and worthwhile pursuit, but we also want you to be engaged. This engagement could include exploring passions and developing new ones and also feeling a part of a community, a small social circle, or even an intimate relationship. Over the next twenty-four hours, diagnose what's missing from your life in terms of engagement. This deficit could be tactile, intellectual, social, or a combination of many factors. What could make your After-50s existence more engaging? What could get you excited about getting up in the morning? Jot down ideas on this front so when you arrive at Part 4, you'll be ready to generate momentum.

- **List things you'd like less of.** You don't have to always add things to build momentum. Think of a reality show about hoarders. The star of the show is always the wise organizer who liberates the hoarder by guiding them to purge unneeded items. The hope is that these acts will build a feng shui-like momentum that will linger after the show moves on. We bet you have some unwanted metaphorical clutter in your After-50s life. It certainly could be material, but often it involves obligations. Some of these obligations may be to dependent family members. All we want you to do over the next twenty-four hours is list burdens you'd like to decrease. You may be tired of mowing your lawn every five days or the obligation of preparing a large meal every evening. Only you can decide if you are comfortable stepping away from certain obligations, but listing those burdens is an important step.

BUILDING MOMENTUM

To successfully embrace the Momentum Mindset, you'll need to also embrace the concept of incrementalism that we shared earlier in this Hack. We After-50s are not as adaptive as we once were. You may have learned this the hard way when you took note of how long it now takes you to heal—from anything. We get it because we're in the same boat. So with everything you take on that is new, or anything you're trying to return to, be patient. While you're dabbling in these new pursuits, make sure to acknowledge growth. This growth, like your healing, may be modest, slow, and nonlinear—two steps forward; one step back—but over the long term, this growth will be substantial.

Step 1: Welcome obstacles.

You have probably experienced plenty of occasions when you've been unsuccessful in your pursuit of a goal. Think about a few of those failures. The examples can be from back in your murky past. What caused the setbacks? When you evaluate these setbacks in terms of why they weren't successful and how you could learn from them, you have the potential to morph into a highly adaptive momentum-builder. We previously used the word "adaptive" regarding incrementalism. We alluded to diminishing adaptivity in general as we age. If we start to embrace setbacks as instructive and enlightening, though, we could potentially become more growth-oriented than when we were young. We can state unequivocally that we have learned more from our defeats than from our victories. Those failures didn't seem like blessings at the time, but they sure turned out to be. You may find yourself to be highly adaptive if you embrace this paradigm.

Step 2: Assume a *Why not me?* disposition.

Sadly, a lot of After-50s don't feel capable or even worthy. Some feel that their best days are behind them and their talents and gifts are dwindling. While it would be irrational to claim that you are the same person you were twenty years ago, perhaps you are now a better version of yourself. You are more experienced, more rational, and hopefully more empathetic. When you've experienced as much as you have, it creates an inclination to more enlightened decision-making. We confess that we often cringe when we think of some of our hormone-fueled decisions when we were stricken by the arrogance of youth. After-50s can leverage all their life experiences to achieve their goals. And, go ahead and assume the disposition that you're as entitled to happiness as any other person on this planet. Why not you? You're just as special as everyone else.

Step 3: Don't worry about looking silly.

This is not just great advice for After-50s; this is a solid aspiration regardless of age. When you try new things, you may look and feel silly. This is not the end of the world. You may have been a CEO, but that does not mean that you can breakdance, hula-hoop, or speak French. But when you don't try new things because you fear the impact on your perceived image, the opportunity cost (there's some CEO lingo) is enormous. You may miss making a new friend as you both try to slobber through your first French sentence. You may miss laughing so hard that your spouse becomes concerned for your health when you try to hula-hoop to build your core muscles and enhance your mobility. You may miss being exposed to incredible new music when you challenge your offspring to show you how to execute a contemporary dance in the family room. If you try new things and look silly, you won't spoil your reputation. You'll probably transform into a wonderful role model for your kids. They'll need to be adventurous when they get older too. They'll be more inclined to do so if they see you as unafraid to try things. And yes, you probably will look silly.

Step 4: Focus your efforts.

An old adage says that when you try to do everything, you end up doing nothing. That is a danger. It is exciting to embrace a Momentum Mindset, and you need to aim your momentum in one direction. Focus on just a few goals to start. As suggested in the What You Can Do Tomorrow section, strive toward a physical well-being goal, an emotional well-being goal, and an engagement goal. Improving your life in these three areas would constitute a major renovation project. As the adage suggests, if you are too scattered in your goals, monitoring growth will seem impossible. Select one objective that you're passionate about and pursue it.

> *"Most sane people would much rather be at home and in bed at 8 a.m. on a Monday than at their jobs or sitting in a classroom. I would instead morph myself into a positive and energetic presence in my students' lives. I would smile and greet them. I would ask about their weekends. I'd introduce the lesson dramatically. Was it a bit contrived? Yes. Was it worth it? Definitely! It improved the atmosphere in my class each Monday, and often my elevated moods became a self-fulfilling prophecy for me and a bit infectious for my students."*

Step 5: Go on tangents and welcome spontaneity.

This advice may seem to completely contradict the previous step. When you pursue a goal, you may get sidetracked. That's okay. Perhaps your original goal lacked clarity or you found another path that is much more interesting. Maybe pursuing your original goal was not as fulfilling as you had hoped. When you pursue intentions, scenic bypasses will present themselves. We go on detours all the time. Many of these detours have enriched our lives profoundly. If an old goal begins to lose its sway on you and an interesting new goal appears in your side view, go for it. Please remember, you create your goals to serve you, not the opposite. There's no obligation. Additionally, once you start embracing a Momentum Mindset, new exploration options will materialize out of thin air. You may venture to the library to pick up a book on how to incorporate resistance training into your fitness routine. This excursion could have been inspired by your goal to improve your physical well-being.

Upon entering the library, you notice on the bulletin board a flier advertising a wine-tasting class on Tuesday nights. You've always been interested in taking such a class, and why not? Such a class may lead to your engagement objectives of meeting local, like-minded After-50s.

REMOVING OBSTACLES

Thankfully, we age slowly. We may not notice the significant changes we've undergone until we're confronted by an old photograph that we haven't seen in years. Or, we greet a long-lost friend and barely recognize them. If you were to dump your twenty-year-old self into your After-50s body, your younger self would probably be shocked. But that's not the way aging works. We often comment about how good and vibrant we feel. Our younger selves would probably not be impressed with our current status. This incrementalism is ultimately a blessing. But you also must adjust your view of momentum. Setting goals and achieving them will look different at this stage of life. Watch out for these obstacles, and address them.

I find myself lost in nostalgia. We can relate. This is a natural response to the aging process. It's so easy to hark back to the good old days when you were like a supple sapling. Such longings, though, don't serve you if they prevent you from living now. What's more, harping about how great the old days were is a total drag for the younger folks in your life. In general, they have no idea what you're talking about because they have no source of reference.

You are a citizen of the present. Live here and now. Instead of reminiscing, leverage nostalgia to serve you. When you think about your younger self, don't just think of the glories but think also of the setbacks. What can you learn from your younger self? As you embark on new experiences, leverage memories of past life adventures to make you more successful now.

I'm not optimistic about my future. As we outlined early in this Hack, we're all headed down the same mortal path. Aging is natural. All the young, energetic, mentally sharp people in your life now will be where you are if they are lucky enough to live as long as you have. Please don't miss wonderful opportunities that life has to offer now because you're so fixated on your mortality—perhaps many decades ahead. Instead, enjoy your life now. Embrace the Momentum Mindset and try something new. You can live like you will be around for a long time. Take full advantage of what life in this stage has to offer.

> *"As someone who suffers from epilepsy, which has a life expectancy about ten years lower than average, I used to worry that I would miss out on a decade or more of time with my family and friends. This worry, as with most worries, is stressful and debilitating. Now, my Momentum Mindset has me living in the now, taking great care of myself, and enjoying daily life. I can't control my own mortality, and I'm planning to beat the odds."*

I'm not wired this way. All this optimism of the Momentum Mindset seems manufactured. On this front, we do have to confess some guilt. We are promoting an idea that some may see as a bit labored. We don't want you to be phony; we do want you to be positive. And in some cases, this means that you have to talk yourself into optimism. We surmise that you've experienced the opposite. If you dread going to the neighborhood barbecue, you'll be hard-pressed to have fun there. Sometimes you have to fake it till you make it and talk yourself into having a good time. Sometimes you just have to boldly go where you haven't gone before. You have a better chance of succeeding in this new endeavor if you consider success as an option, at least, and as an expected result, at best.

I'm not adventurous. When we encourage pursuing ambitious goals with a Momentum Mindset, some folks get the wrong idea. They might conjure up images of running a marathon, skydiving, or setting up an internet dating profile. These are certainly audacious activities, and if you're game to take on these challenges—bravo! But your adventures should be thrilling to you, and they certainly don't have to be impressive to others. We suggest creating and then pursuing goals that are engaging and meaningful to you. You've earned it. So, be adventurous, even if it's in your own quiet way. You do you!

THE HACK IN ACTION

Throughout this Hack, we've advanced the idea that momentum may look different after the age of fifty. Your objectives may be more modest, or they may be unlike your past choices. Your goals may be ostentatious or subtle. But whatever you apply the Momentum Mindset to must resonate with you and serve you. The heck with achieving goals to impress others; this is your time.

Jim's story ...

In the past five years, my wife and I both retired. We taught in public schools for decades. We loved that life. Those who teach don't get monetarily rich, but we are not materialistic. We invested well and systematically. We owe just a bit on our mortgage but otherwise have no debt. Even though we set ourselves up well, our income declined once we stopped working full time. We both have part-time jobs that we enjoy, and each helps close the income gap created by our smaller pensions. But we are not spend-thrifts. We invest a lot in travel, home improvement projects, and entertaining friends and family, and we also invest in our fitness. We've been successful living this fulfilling After-50s existence without tapping into our investments. We don't see this situation changing.

None of this would be the case, however, if we hadn't taken positive steps and then built off those decisions—the Momentum Mindset. After retirement, our earning patterns changed, so we needed to adjust our spending. Some of it happened organically. Our tender offspring became largely financially independent. We're empty nesters, which means a lot less of our resources are devoted to food and transportation. We're no longer sending tuition checks. Our commuting costs have diminished, and we rarely spend on professional clothing.

In our big post-working budget planning sit-down, we were pleased that our diminished obligations largely offset our loss of income, but we weren't satisfied. We slowly applied a Momentum Mindset to our financial retirement balance sheet. One of our first decisions was to designate money for big-ticket items. We need to purchase a new car in the next few years. We don't like financing depreciating assets. We decided to take my retirement severance and purchase the car with cash.

Our second big decision was how we would purchase travel experiences and home improvement projects. We decided to use our part-time working income and combine it with the royalties we earn from my books, which is inconsistent but can occasionally be robust.

Our third big decision was about becoming more frugal with our discretionary spending. We set up a monthly allowance allotment for each of us. We know—it's like we are teenagers again. This has worked well for us. When we do purchase, we purchase quality, but we just don't need as much stuff—we probably never did. We also play offense. We use fuel points and coupons. We've turned into promotional code inserters. We sometimes delay purchases in a self-imposed cooling-off period. We will put items on our Amazon Wish List. If we still want it two weeks later, it wasn't an impulse buy.

Our greatest coup is with our grocery rewards fuel

points. When both of our cars are nearly empty, we'll drive separately to the filling station. We do this during less busy times so other customers don't get mad. My wife will pull up to the pump, and I pull in right behind her. She'll fill her tank, and then we take turns holding the pump while we play musical chairs with our cars. By not ending the purchase after she's filled her tank, we still take advantage of the fuel points for my car too. How's that for an After-50s weekday morning adventure?

Each of these steps has built off the other—momentum. One could look at this and think it seems like a life of sacrifice. But we are less concerned with what others may think of our fiscal plans; we have embraced this experience as an engaging game.

Embracing a Momentum Mindset makes life more fun, engaging, fulfilling, exciting, and adaptable. We could go on with more adjectives, but we won't. You get the picture.

PART 2

PHYSICAL WELL-BEING

MASTER MEAL PLANNING

Create a personal eating plan that leads to a long, healthy, joy-filled life

*Take care of your body. It's the
only place you have to live.*
— JIM ROHN, AUTHOR AND ENTREPRENEUR

THE PROBLEM: THE SAD DIET MAY BE KILLING YOU

WE WERE BOTH fascinated by a 1948 video that featured pedestrians walking along the streets of New York City. This time capsule featured everyday New Yorkers of all ages, shapes, and ethnicities. This was not a staged performance, and these were not actors. While the clothing styles were impressive (people used to dress up back then), what mesmerized us was how slim the people looked. It was nearly impossible to find an overweight person. Understand that WWII had been over for three years; this was not a time of rationing, and still, people generally appeared healthier than most folks do today.

As you consider this, conduct a contemporary experiment the next time you're out and about, and observe common, everyday people gathering—like at a grocery store or a sporting event. They probably don't look like their ancestors from 1948. Many people today, both old and young, are noticeably heavy and out of shape. We haven't handled this age of abundance well. We were not meant to eat ourselves into oblivion, and we need to make changes.

We can almost hear your heavy sigh and read your mind. After seeing this Problem, you're thinking, *Oh no, these guys are going to promote some fad diet and tell me I have to stop eating everything I love.* Not at all. We are going to talk about nutrition; we're not here, though, to stump for those popular, strict diets you constantly hear about. We will strongly urge you to abandon one diet—the one that might be killing you.

The Standard American Diet (SAD) consists of the kinds of foods that make America one of the most obese countries in the world, with more than 40 percent of people over forty considered to be overweight. If you didn't already do the math, that's a whopping four out of ten Americans. Wondering if you consume too many SAD foods? If you frequent fast-food drive-thrus, spend much of your time at the local grocery in the soda and potato chip aisles, and top off nightly dinners with sugary desserts, you are eating from the SAD menu, and this sad fact has to change, to some degree, if you want to feel better.

"So, I'm a little overweight," you may say. "What's the big deal?" Even though we use obesity to emphasize the deleterious effects of the SAD, the problem isn't so much about your weight or your shape as it is about your overall health. The bigger concern is life-threatening diseases, like cancer, Type 2 diabetes, heart disease, and stroke. According to the Centers for Disease Control and Prevention (CDC), many of these frightening ailments are caused by poor nutrition—more specifically, foods that are high in sodium (think sandwiches and pizza), cholesterol (think deep-fried foods), and refined carbohydrates (think breads, pasta, and sugary desserts and beverages). In addition to the aforementioned lethal diseases, diets high in sodium and refined carbohydrates have been linked to dementia and Alzheimer's. Additionally, SAD foods are high in fat and sugar, which, according to a 2023 study by Uppsala University researchers, negatively impact deep sleep and oscillatory patterns (brain waves that impact sleep regularity). We take a deep dive into the value of sleep in Hack 7.

So, how do you get off this SAD train? It's easier than you think, and we've got a Hack to get you started.

THE HACK: BECOME A MASTER MEAL PLANNER

If you're like most people, you've lived your life enjoying food, rarely considering how you eat, or constantly battling weight problems and trying every fad diet available in order to fit into a new outfit or coax your physique into looking a certain way. As you get older, your body will talk to you in ways it didn't when you were in your twenties and thirties. You may groan when you get out of a chair or bend over to tie your shoes. You might notice aches and stiffness in your back and joints that didn't bother you in the past. In some cases, you might think these issues are weight related. Chances are, they have less to do with your weight and more to do with how you eat.

The beauty of this Hack is that, unlike proponents of fad diets, we won't suggest one solution. We won't say you should eat or drink only X and cut out all of Y. The key to a joyful After-50s life, we believe, is to find the right balance, and to do this, you need to create a diet that keeps you happy while reducing the aches and pains that the SAD diet brings. We encourage this way of eating because that's what the scientific community promotes. Other approaches exist, but we are inclined to follow what the medical community says. Eating a mostly plant-based diet is ideal, although it is difficult and unappealing for many, so we want you to make your own diet—one that includes more fruits and vegetables. Let us reiterate that we're not saying you should give up all the foods you love. We believe in balance. In other words, we want you to discover the balanced diet that works for you, keeping in mind that the Standard American Diet does not work for anyone.

"Penny is sixty and fit. Many who meet her are surprised that she is not younger. Once they get to know her, however, they are even more amazed when it's revealed that she has a fountain Pepsi fetish. Penny understands the negative impact of this vice, so she limits her interaction with this bad boy by slurping only one Pepsi per week. She revels in this weekly carbonated indulgence, but because she drinks it so infrequently, she dulls any negative impact."

To master meal planning, you need to know the kinds of foods that fight the diseases that ruin an After-50s life and can ultimately kill you, like heart disease, diabetes, dementia, obesity, cancer, and others. Then, you must learn how to incorporate these disease-fighting foods into daily meals in a way that doesn't make you feel like you're on a diet. Just as the Standard American Diet kills, fad diets also fail because most people abandon diets shortly after starting them. When you are a master meal planner, healthy eating becomes an adventure. We include a few healthy and unhealthy choices here, and you can always find other lists with a simple Google search. Just be sure you're relying on credible sources—ideally, those with content that is written by or reviewed by doctors or licensed nutritionists.

WHAT YOU CAN DO TOMORROW

As a master meal planner, you will create an eating plan that keeps you fit and enjoying your After-50s lifestyle. Here are some actions you can take starting tomorrow.

- **Eat more fruits and vegetables.** The first step many fad diets recommend is to morph into a vegetarian, a vegan, or simply to eat only fruits and vegetables. While this kind of eating would certainly make you feel better, it can scare the bejesus out of people who struggle to consume a variety of vegetables and/or love their meats. Remember, one of our favorite words is "balance." A fun and easy way to integrate fruits and vegetables into your diet, which most doctors agree is a must for health and longevity, is to drink them in a delicious smoothie or mix them into something else you already enjoy. If you have a blender, toss in dark greens (spinach is super healthy and pretty mild tasting), mixed berries, a half banana, and some water, Greek yogurt, flavored kefir, or coconut milk into a cup and blend.

Pro Tip: For a cold, frothy smoothie, add ice or freeze your smoothie mix before adding liquid and blending. If this sounds like too much work, try sautéing some greens, onions, cauliflower, peppers, and mushrooms—or any combination that you can tolerate. Then, mix these into an omelet or a whole-grain wrap. Feel free to add salsa or a tasty balsamic or red wine vinegar. Try this a few times a week; we think you'll start loving it before you know it.

- **Eliminate one SAD food or drink.** Pause your reading for about twenty seconds, grab a pen and pad, and jot down everything you'll eat and drink today, tomorrow, and over the course of the next week. Consider the parts of your diet that are poor choices (we listed some in The Problem section). Now, choose one thing to eliminate, starting as soon as tomorrow. This doesn't mean you have to cut it completely from your diet. Say, for example, you drink one or two cans of soda several days per week, or maybe you down a doughnut or a bagel on your way to work. Cut those drinks or doughnuts for one or more days. After a week or two, add another day or cut another unhealthy food. This strategy is not nearly as challenging as you think; plus, it will instantly make you feel better and could add years to your life.

- **Drink more water.** According to the National Library of Medicine, about half the world's population drinks less than the minimum recommended daily amount of water—about 1.5 liters, or 51 fluid ounces (remember, this is the minimum amount you need). Water is your most natural resource for helping regulate body temperature, transport nutrients, lubricate your joints, curb hunger, and more. (Skeptical? Ask your doctor about the impact of water on your health.) While the health profession varies on how much water to consume, you can start with the old standby: drink eight glasses every day. Remember, sodas, lattes, and alcoholic beverages don't count. Your master meal planner—that's you—recommends water. Grab a glass now.

- **Find something new for your refrigerator or cupboard.** Learning how to master meal planning is an amazing journey filled with exploration, research, conversation, shopping, and joy. Start this journey by adding one new, healthy food or beverage to your kitchen. If you are a snacker, consider swapping out chips, candy, or that latte for an option you would not usually choose. A few of our favorites include mixed nuts, blueberries, an apple, no-butter popcorn, dark chocolate, and herbal tea. Check your spice rack (don't worry if you don't have one). Herbs and spices not only add taste to what some people consider to be bland foods (think vegetables), but they also play a huge role in health and longevity. Cinnamon fights inflammation and lowers cholesterol. Cayenne pepper reduces appetite. Rosemary helps with nasal congestion, and saffron has been linked to reduced anxiety and depression.

BUILDING MOMENTUM

Now, a few chapters in, you're likely finding that the What You Can Do Tomorrow strategies in each Hack simplify changes that can seem, at first glance, overwhelming. The more difficult part is taking those right-now ideas and turning them into monthlong, yearlong, or even lifelong habits. Here are a few steps to help you build momentum toward turning right-now dietary changes into long-term, life-sustaining habits.

Step 1: Talk to your doctor.

When Mark battled long-haul COVID—a story we share later in this chapter's Hack in Action—he made important changes to his diet, which he discussed with his doctor. We can't emphasize enough the importance of consulting your physician about changes to your diet. Remember, we are not doctors or licensed nutritionists. We're just a couple of well-researched practitioners of health, fitness, and longevity; we know what works well for us. When creating a balanced meal plan that is right for you, your doctor can play an instrumental role. She literally knows you inside and out. While broccoli is one of the most nutritious greens you can find, packed with fiber and antioxidants, it is not right for everyone. If you suffer from irritable bowel syndrome, for example, your doctor might tell you to avoid broccoli. Plus, your doctor can be a resource beyond those we provide in this book, pointing you in the direction of superfoods that will be perfect for *your* body.

Step 2: Make your old bad eating habits difficult.

Many people who exist on SAD food have habits that set them up to fail. They spend too much time in the wrong aisles of the grocery store. Their commute takes them on the road to irresistible fast-food restaurants or coffee shops. They keep huge containers of flour, sugar, and the wrong kinds of oils in their cupboards. They inadvertently buy the wrong "healthy" snacks (think cereal, granola bars, pretzels, and rice cakes). Make these choices difficult with a few potentially easy changes. Try to find a different route to work or the salon—one that bypasses your favorite fast-food stops. Steer your cart past the wrong aisles when shopping, avoiding your go-to high-sugar or carb-packed snacks. When considering healthy snacks, be sure to read labels or do a little research before buying (avoid ingredients like sucrose, fructose, sucralose, and corn syrup, which are sugars and artificial sweeteners). Discard SAD foods immediately; yes, throw them out. You'll thank us later.

"For years, my go-to snack was a cereal bar, which I thought was a healthy choice. After learning to read the fine print, I realized that these tiny treats contained little protein and fiber (the good stuff) while packing tons of sugar and salt into 190 calories. They no longer exist in my cupboard, and I don't miss them one bit."

Step 3: Make lunch or dinner a mysterious and fun adventure.

After some research into the kinds of food and beverages that can improve your health and lead to a longer life, start planning some adventurous meals with a significant other. Pick an afternoon or evening without distraction.

Pro Tip: Put your mobile devices away. Turn on some of your favorite music and dim the lights; maybe burn some candles. Then, prepare your new meal together, anticipating a delightful experience that you will share with someone special. When you equate a dietary change with joy and companionship, it will be easy to eat more healthy meals and build momentum for a new way of eating.

Step 4: Indulge.

Pick one day each week that you and your significant other will abandon your healthy diet and go crazy (okay, maybe not completely crazy). The fad diets that we hate tend to call this a "cheat day." Taking a day to indulge is part of your new dietary plan; we don't consider this cheating. When you make a balanced meal plan, you eat mostly nutrient-rich, plant-based, healthy foods. Occasionally, you tantalize your taste buds with your favorite unhealthy foods. We love pizza and enjoy a few slices with our spouses weekly. Maybe once a month, we'll grab some chicken wings and a beer or two with friends. Remember, the key is balance.

Pro Tip: Once you've built momentum toward a healthy

lifestyle, use the 80/20 rule—80 percent of your meals are mostly plant-based, including some superfoods, and 20 percent are your old favorites.

Super Pro Tip: When eating an unhealthy meal, put down your fork after each bite; this will keep you from gorging yourself on that favorite food.

REMOVING OBSTACLES

Changing your diet—or as we prefer, creating a new way of eating—is tough for anyone. Here are potential *what ifs* that may be swirling around in your brain, with suggestions for removing these obstacles.

What if I've battled weight problems my whole life? For full transparency, we can't empathize with this real and very personal issue, and we won't diminish what is surely a serious obstacle for you. It's also important to remember that this Hack is not focused on weight; this is about health and longevity. Our best advice is for you to follow the strategies in this chapter, starting with cutting out at least one SAD food. After cutting out a refined carb (think white bread, pastas, and sodas), try replacing it with some leafy greens, whole grains, legumes (think spinach, quinoa, and black beans), and fresh water. Remember, one of the best ways to integrate plant-based foods is by making it an adventure, shared with someone you love.

What if I hate vegetables? Many people who say they hate vegetables were inadvertently programmed early in life that veggies are bad. Perhaps their parents didn't eat or serve vegetables, or if they did, their go-to was broccoli, cauliflower, or cabbage—perhaps steamed or boiled. Dessert came at the end of meals and, in many cases, only after eating the vegetables. This well-intentioned, albeit poorly executed, plan made many people learn that veggies were downright evil. Kids want food that tantalizes their taste buds. It's never too late, though, to learn to love vegetables (and don't forget fruit). Start by preparing them in a way that enhances the taste. Try frying some spinach and onion in extra virgin olive oil (a healthy fat), add a little pepper or other tasty spice (cinnamon is a fabulous choice), and fold the veggies into an omelet. You can find many ways to prepare vegetables and mix them into other foods you enjoy. Check out one of the many cooking shows on your favorite streaming channel for ideas.

What if I'm too busy to prepare food? Thanks in large part to a pandemic, the delivery business exploded and continues to thrive. Couple this with an increase in restaurants focusing on healthy foods and subscription services that will deliver healthy choices weekly or monthly, and it's pretty easy to master your eating plan.

What if I hate water? We know many people who flatly refuse water, preferring coffee, tea, or soda. In various places in this book, we endorse the use of technology. One way to drink more water is to make it a competition with a friend or family member or just with yourself. Search for a mobile app that helps you easily log your water intake, or keep a water journal. Some apps have default amounts like 4 ounces, 8 ounces, and 16 ounces. You just tap what you drank, and the app logs it and adds up the total each day. If eight 10-ounce glasses seem impossible, start with 4 ounces (just a couple of quick chugs). You can down twenty of these tiny waters with ease.

Pro Tip: Add flavor to your water with some fruit—a slice of lemon, a squeeze of lime, or a few berries.

What if my family thinks I don't need to change how I eat? One simple answer is to ask them to read this book or at least share some of its key takeaways. We'd recommend presenting dietary changes as a long journey rather than an abrupt, drastic change. Assure your small community that you are not forcing anything on them. Explain that you want to live a long, healthy, adventurous life that you want to share with them. Part of this adventure is taking on new challenges and trying new things. Set a goal for yourself and invite loved ones to help you by sharing the journey. Importantly, provide a lengthy menu of food choices and invite everyone to participate in selecting ingredients for meals. The great news about being an After-50 is that your days of satisfying multiple palates could be limited. Meal prep is a lot easier when you're an empty nester.

THE HACK IN ACTION

Mark was always athletic. He ran track and cross country in college and could hold his own with younger competitors on the basketball and tennis courts. A few years into his After-50s life, though, Mark realized he was slowing down more than he'd expected. The arthritis in his lower back and bursitis in his left shoulder became more noticeable each year. Diagnosed with epilepsy at thirty-three, he has been managing the disease with medication for decades and remains seizure-free. Still, the side effects of anti-seizure medication come with mood swings, fatigue, and dizziness. At one point, Mark decided to make dietary changes in an attempt to mitigate these side effects and feel more energetic. Then he contracted COVID-19, and his health situation got worse.

Mark's story ...

When my two kids hit their late teens, I realized it wouldn't be long until my wife and I would be empty nesters. While this dramatic life change was frightening, I realized that the next chapter could be as good, maybe better, than the first, as long as I felt good. Fast food, potato chips, and sweets were a big part of my diet, but because I was never diagnosed as obese, I rarely considered the foods I ate. My foray into healthy eating started with smoothies. Mollie had been a smoothie enthusiast for years, and I figured the smoothie could be an easy way to inject fruits and vegetables into my diet. After about a month of experimenting with various concoctions, I discovered a blend I truly enjoyed, and I started feeling a little less fatigue (which was a big side effect of my medication). Soon, I was cutting back on cheeseburgers, chicken wings, and fries. In 2021, I lost nearly twenty-five pounds. I felt more like thirty-seven than fifty-seven.

In December of that year, I was hit hard by COVID. While I wasn't hospitalized and I overcame the worst symptoms in about a week, I suffered from long-haul COVID for many months. This included horrible fatigue (some days, it was difficult to walk from one room to the next), poor focus, throat pain, insomnia, memory loss, and other mental problems. Doctors had few answers for this mystifying disease, which affects tens of millions of Americans. In early 2022, with my long-term health in question, I needed to take action.

The small dietary changes I'd made the prior year had me feeling great prior to contracting COVID, and I believed a more rigid nutrition plan was in order. I created an eating plan that, coupled with pacing, meditation, and breathing exercises, I believed would help me overcome, or at least manage, my COVID symptoms. I started by ramping up the already-nutrient-rich smoothie I drank daily and adding collagen powder, flaxseed, and kefir milk to my go-to mix of spinach, mixed berries, and bananas. I upped my water intake to more than three liters every day—100–140 ounces. These additions would strengthen my immune system, increase muscle mass, and support heart health, which is a concern for all COVID long-haulers.

Next, I cut back on meat, limiting my weekly meals to a few servings of fish and chicken. While I cut back on snacks, when I did indulge, I replaced cereal bars and string cheese with handfuls of mixed nuts, blueberries, and dark chocolate. These gave me the boost I needed to avoid too much sitting or napping while continuing to give my body the fuel it needed to move a little more each day.

When I started feeling better, I realized that I had become a master meal planner, and my way of eating became a wonderful, healthy lifestyle that I never want to change.

While this book outlines ideas for living a great life after fifty, you can find many more ideas if you look for them. Start with small changes. And, as it did with Mark, mastering your meal plan will not only put you on a wonderful, joy-filled journey, but it also might help you defeat diseases and inflammation-related ailments while adding years to your life.

Hack 4

MOVE

Purposefully introduce more movement into your life

A body in motion stays in motion.
— Isaac Newton, mathematician

THE PROBLEM: MOST ADULTS DON'T MOVE ENOUGH

Accumulating to the Centers for Disease Control and Prevention, 25 percent of American adults are sedentary. We don't move enough. In fact, with the advent of remote work, thanks in large part to COVID, many of us find ourselves rarely leaving our homes. Add in retired After-50s, and you have one more recipe for sedentary hermithood. Not moving is bad for you. And you don't need to take our word for it. Two decades ago, the World Health Organization warned in a newsletter that "Physical Inactivity Is a Leading Cause of Disease and Disability." A more contemporary exhortation to move comes from the *British Journal of Sports Medicine*. The creators of a comprehensive study on the impact of walking merely eleven minutes a day found it makes a profound impact on avoiding an early fatal cardiac event. Cardiovascular disease is the world's number one cause of death. We'll talk more about the potential of walking.

We After-50s simply must move more. The more we move, the better we do it, the better it feels, and the more positive the impact. Unless, of course, you overdo it and get injured. We've both done that, too.

But here's another problem when it comes to movement: many After-50s up their movement game based on elusive objectives. We've heard friends say, "I want to lose weight, so I'm going to start jogging" (or biking, swimming, dancing, or doing hot yoga). We're all for you embarking on any of these quests. And doing such activities will help you lose fat, but unfortunately, perhaps not as much as you had hoped.

Your body converts the food you eat into energy. This process is referred to as metabolism. It seems like a simplistic process with two variables—input food, output movement. You could manipulate either variable or both, and you should get predictable results. Eat less and get thinner. Move more and get thinner. But metabolism is complicated. It's possible for runners to be overweight. One would think that all that activity would zap body fat, but much to the chagrin of cardio devotees everywhere, it doesn't. And the fact that these activities are collectively referred to as cardio (exercise for your heart) should be a clear indicator of what part of the body is primarily benefiting.

If you do a deep dive into how metabolism functions, you'll quickly realize that it behaves like a vast symphony with many components. Your metabolism's purpose is to keep your brain and heart functioning, and everything else, for that matter, so you can take your next breath or fight off your next cold. Your metabolism devotes the vast majority of your food consumption to keeping you alive. Melting your love handles is far down your metabolism's to-do list. As far as your metabolism is concerned, those precious love handles are like the Strategic Oil Reserve and can be used to give you energy in an emergency. Yep, your metabolism is a bit paranoid.

So if you're out for a jog and considering running one more mile, or you decide to take a walk after dinner, or you take up yoga or tai chi, or you get up from your desk and do a few air squats—have at it. Just don't be discouraged if this effort has a marginal impact on your waistline. It'll help, but probably not as much as you had hoped. There's an accurate saying in the fitness community: *You can't outrun a bad diet.* Life would be so much simpler if this weren't true.

But guess what? All of the movement choices we just advertised are still good for you. They will help some if your goal is to lose weight, but they can significantly improve your overall health. Movement will also make you feel more vibrant. This Hack will give you a new appreciation for the magic of movement.

THE HACK: GET MOVING

Doctor Mike Young is the director of performance and sports science at Athletic Lab. In an impactful 2022 TED Talk, he boldly stated that *movement is medicine*. We love this label. Dr. Young argues that movement is a highly effective treatment for virtually every catastrophic illness that afflicts After-50s, including cognitive disorders. What's more, movement is free, portable, and has limited, controllable, and predictable side effects.

When it comes to movement, After-50s have vast options. We'll explore some in this Hack, but please find your own movement path. Neither of us does ballroom dancing, but *you* certainly can. At this juncture, it's important to distinguish between two movement goals. One is to improve cardiovascular health, and the other is to improve mobility— the ability to move freely and easily through an expanding range of motion. There's plenty of spillover with most forms of movement. When you walk briskly to elevate your heart rate, you'll also improve your mobility. When you take a tai chi class to improve your mobility and balance, you'll also elevate your heart rate. The diverse benefits that come with most forms of movement are wonderful. One programming note: we're so passionate about resistance training that we devote Hack 5 to that form of movement, so we won't talk about it in this one.

The Centers for Disease Control and Prevention suggests a weekly goal of 150 minutes of moderate-intensity activity, or seventy-five minutes of vigorous activity. Moderate activity could include walking briskly or bike riding, while examples of vigorous activity (movement that elevates your heart rate significantly) would be jogging, swimming laps, and resistance training. The 150 or seventy-five minutes are not magic thresholds. As previously mentioned, the *British Journal of Sports Medicine* advocates the cascading health benefits of walking just eleven minutes every day. If you follow the *British Journal's* recommendation and take an eleven-minute walk after dinner, you'll rack up seventy-seven minutes of moderate-intensity activity in a week. That's slightly over halfway to the CDC's goal. If you increase your time investment to twenty-two minutes each day or enhance the intensity of your movement choices, the CDC and your primary care provider will (or should) award you a gold star. You can do this!

> *"I used to struggle to find time to walk just for the sake of walking. I was too busy doing anything else. Now, I break up various activities with short walks—eight to twelve minutes around my neighborhood or in the woods. I do five to eight of these brisk strolls daily and absolutely love it."*

Let's plan more movement today, this week, and every day going forward. This Hack will expose you to options and strategies. The goal is simply to move more, and we'll explore subtle opportunities to make valuable deposits into your movement bank.

WHAT YOU CAN DO TOMORROW

- **Calculate your resting heart rate.** Your resting heart rate is how often your heart beats in one minute when you're completely relaxed, like when you wake up. Measure this first thing tomorrow morning. Many wearable fitness devices will do this for you. To do it without the aid of technology, the Mayo Clinic recommends feeling your pulse and counting the beats over a fifteen-second period while you are at rest (not immediately after exercise or other exertion). Then, multiply that number of beats by four to get a sixty-second resting heart rate. This figure is important because you want your resting heart rate to decrease over time. The American Heart Association states that a resting heart rate of between sixty to one hundred beats is normal. Athletes tend to fall below sixty beats, and as you start moving more, a decreasing resting heart rate could be a valuable metric to demonstrate your improving heart health.

- **Calculate your target heart rate.** This data range will create a movement intensity goal. Take the number 220 and subtract your age. This will give you your maximum heart rate. This is how fast your heart should pound during your most intense movement efforts. If you are sixty-two, your maximum heart rate will be 158 beats per minute. According to the American Heart Association, your exercise sweet spot is between 50 to 85 percent of your maximum heart rate. For our sixty-two-year-old example, that equates to a target heart rate of between 79 and 134 beats per minute. Try measuring your pulse today immediately after your movement effort. The target heart rate is cumbersome to assess because you need to measure your pulse immediately after an effort. For efficiency and accuracy, measure it for fifteen seconds and then multiply that number by four. Take this measure every week or so. What you'll hopefully find is that your target heart rate zone is being maintained while your intensity of effort has increased as you've become fitter. That's a magnificent sign of progress.

Pro Tip: Invest in wearable technology that measures both resting heart rate and your heart rate after exercise. Some of these devices are quite accurate and even track your heart rate averages over time.

- **Plan morning movement.** Obviously, this is contingent upon your daily schedule. If you crawl out of bed at the last minute and rush off to work, you're going to have to get up a bit earlier or carve out a break in the morning to accomplish this. But if you work from home or are retired, you have the freedom to pull this off. Our aim is to stack up weekly movement minutes each morning like cordwood. Some days, we run, or practice strength training, or do a yoga session, or perform other movement options like a barre class. We typically do an early morning mobility routine prior to these more dramatic movements. But many days, we merely walk. Taking a brisk walk in the morning is magical. Not only is it a solid cardio option, but it's also great for you cognitively and emotionally. Moreno Zugaro, a men's coach, argues in an article titled "5 Common Habits That Kill

Your Drive, Motivation, and Energy" that a morning walk in the sunlight releases stress, enhances alertness for the remainder of the day, and sets up your circadian rhythm for a wonderful night's sleep. Choose a form of movement that appeals to you, and do it tomorrow morning.

"When I walk is when I learn. I typically listen to a podcast or audiobook on my morning walks. Sometimes I get so engrossed that I walk for longer than I planned. My mind is ultra-receptive in the morning. I've grown to love this part of the day."

- **Include movement with your coffee break.** You've probably heard the terrifying cliché that *sitting is the new smoking.* This stark comparison rings true. We all sit too much when we work—like composing a manuscript for people over fifty. And that's not even factoring in plopping ourselves on the couch to watch TV each night. Sitting is bad for us. It eliminates mobility, atrophies your heart, and devastates posture. While working, it's totally healthy to take a break from sitting at your monitor, but instead of just migrating to the breakroom or your kitchen table and sitting again to consume a refreshment and do a little dishing with friends, walk a couple of floors or around the block. We especially like this time to execute a few mobility options. To counter all this compression caused by prolonged sitting, perform ten repetitions of the cat-cow stretch, or air squats, or shoulder pass-throughs with a towel, or pigeon poses for your hips. Such movements will feel great, enhance your mobility, and make you more productive when you crawl back in the saddle in front of your computer.

- **Take a twenty-two-minute walk after dinner.** This is our favorite strategy. After you've cleaned up from the meal, take a stroll through your neighborhood. If you commit to this act every evening, you'll reach your weekly 150-minute activity threshold. But the potential of the walk doesn't end with heart health. When you know that a walk will follow dinner, you'll magically self-regulate your consumption. No one wants to take a walk if you're too full to move. A post-dinner walking routine will go a long way toward achieving the elusive goal of portion control. And, if you're like us, you can be accompanied on your evening circuit by a friend, a dog (who probably desperately needs to move too), or a loved one. This will be a marvelous opportunity to bond.

BUILDING MOMENTUM

Now that you're starting to move more, we're hoping it feels great. Moving is natural. Sitting for the entire day is not. In the last section, we championed a movement goal of 150 minutes a week. Once you started inventorying movement, we hope you were impressed with how much movement you were able to accumulate in a week. Let's build on this effort.

Step 1: Consider using a fitness tracker.

We use the word *consider* because we're uncomfortable promoting that you buy anything. But we both use these popular and pretty amazing tools. If you're at all confused about these devices, a fitness tracker is a piece of wearable technology like a watch or a ring that tracks movement and heart rate. Most also provide valuable information on how you're sleeping. There are many variations of these fitness trackers, and they aren't too expensive. Fitbit and Garmin are industry standards, and you can buy a basic tracker, which will include amazing capabilities, for a reasonable price. The Oura Ring is a bit pricier but a nice alternative if you don't like wearing something on your wrist. You can find plenty of other wearable tech options.

These trackers link to an application you can download to your smartphone, tablet, or laptop, which translates information from your wearable device into measurable data about your activities. These impressive devices will tell you at a glance what your resting heart rate is and how many active minutes you've accumulated. You can even monitor how much time you spent in your target heart rate zone. What we love about fitness trackers is that they inspire movement. A UCLA Health study found that those wearing a fitness tracker made greater health strides when they received daily customized text messages about goals and progress. We've seen and experienced, anecdotally, of course, how these trackers inspire movement. While the ten-thousand-steps-per-day fitness tracker gold standard goal is purely arbitrary, step goals do seem to help motivate us to move. We know that if we notice that we've had a dismal step count and it's already three in the afternoon, we're much more inclined to take an evening walk. If buying one of these trackers will help you monitor your progress or inspire you to move more, we say go for it. Our fitness trackers have done both for us.

Step 2: Become a student of movement.

Spend time, maybe spread over days or weeks, researching movement options. Of course, consult with your physician and knowledgeable acquaintances, and social media can be a great resource too. One benefit we love about social media platforms is that when you search for a form of movement, you often get exceptionally fit individuals demonstrating proper form and technique. You also generally see a slew of comments from people who have followed a post's suggestion and given the movement a try. We've gotten outstanding movement ideas from YouTube, Pinterest, Instagram, TikTok, X (formerly known as Twitter), and even Facebook.

The more you search for movement options, the more movement options will navigate your way organically. Typical mobility options include yoga and Pilates, which are wonderful activities, particularly if you can attend a live class and get some coaching and collaboration with classmates. But you'll be impressed with what you find if you go on your favorite social media platform and search for a ten-minute morning mobility routine. We've been profoundly impacted by such searches and been exposed to creative options that we had not thought of before. Our movement repertoires have grown significantly as a result. As soon as any movement routine gets stale, jump on social media and search for new options.

Step 3: Blow past 150 minutes.

Earlier in this Hack, we echoed the directive from the CDC to accumulate 150 minutes of moderately intense movement each week. What we have found, and what you'll discover as well, is that after you start moving more, surpassing this 150-minute threshold is not difficult. For instance, mowing the lawn and landscaping also elevate your heart rate. Those efforts are applied to that 150-minute objective too. We're confident you'll be bolder in your movements. Many modern After-50s are engaged in activities that our parents and grandparents never would've considered. You can run a 5K, a half-marathon, or a full marathon. You can obtain a black belt in martial arts. You can compete in the Senior Olympics. You can improve your mobility until you can touch your toes, perform the splits, or get certified as a yoga instructor. There's a reason we didn't title this Hack *Move for 150 Minutes Each Week*. We don't want to limit you. Movement brings many positives, and we love the way it makes us feel—energized! We're passionate in our belief that mastering this 150-threshold target will motivate you to do even more. Your "more" is for you to create.

Step 4: Leverage movement.

More movement is a recipe for a more fulfilling life. It's sad to hear folks prematurely eliminate themselves from adventures merely because they don't consider themselves physically able. While we all have a shelf life, there's no reason to hop on the exit ramp too soon. A perfect example comes from walking. Once you start feeling more comfortable walking in your neighborhood, plan a hike at a local metro park. Once you master that, travel to a beautiful state park and traverse one of the longer trails. Once you're comfortable with this experience, venture to a national park and spend the weekend in splendor. And this is just an example with walking. You can increase your progress and enjoyment with any form of movement. You can leverage your commitment to movement to not only improve your health and expand your experiences but also to foster and strengthen relationships. All movement options are so much richer and sweeter if you do them with company. If you have a significant other, you can reconnect once you start moving together. If you have grown kids who you don't see enough, take them hiking or rafting, train for a 5K with them, or enroll together in a Zumba class. It's our experience that communication and bonding thrive in the midst of these activities.

REMOVING OBSTACLES

Introducing more movement into your life presents challenges. Here are coping mechanisms for a few typical hurdles. You may have unique challenges that we don't address, but please assume a positive mindset about your potential to adapt or overcome.

Where I live, the weather is frequently not favorable for outdoor activities. We understand. We live in the northeastern portion of the United States. We experience long, cold winters and plenty of rainy days throughout the year. Our response to this concern is twofold. First, remember that movement options are numerous. On days when going outdoors and walking, jogging, swimming, or biking is not an option, choose movement that you can do inside, like walking on a treadmill, jumping rope, following a yoga instructor on YouTube, or devoting the day to mobility and balance routines. This is where doing your research and finding plenty of movement options pay off. Second, we suggest occasionally braving the elements. Bundle up if it's cold and go for a walk. Grab an umbrella if it's raining and take a quick stroll in your neighborhood. If you live where it's oppressively hot, go for a quick jog in the morning while it's still cool. Braving the elements can be exhilarating and give you a wonderful sense of accomplishment.

What if I hurt myself? Please start slowly with gentle movements and gradually migrate to more intense activities. As previously mentioned, we've both had movement injuries that set us back, and we've learned to embrace minor injuries as opportunities. (We know. Sometimes we write things that make you want to slap us.) When you tweak something in movement, it points to a weakness. It could be a muscle imbalance, a movement limitation, or a local muscular weakness. Your health provider may give you rehab exercises to help you recover. Do those, and you can recover from your setback better equipped to handle future movement. Your injury detour could be beneficial in the long term.

I keep comparing my current self to my younger self. Welcome to the club. We can't run as fast as we used to, and we can't do handstands or cartwheels anymore. We can't effortlessly hinge at the waist and touch our toes without stiffness. But guess what? It still feels like we're doing something impressive when we move. It's all relative. When you're older and you're out running, you may feel like you're flying, but you really aren't running nearly as fast as you did in college. No one expects you to run that fast. Instead, take note of the magnificent way you feel when you move. Think about all the positive things that are happening to your body when you move. Think about all the negative things that will happen if you give up and just sit at your computer. Don't let this obstacle influence you. The more you move, the more you'll feel like your younger self—even if you can't run as fast or jump as high.

THE HACK IN ACTION

Jim was a sprinter on his track team in high school. While he wasn't the fastest, he placed in many meets and was an important member of sprint relays. He loved being one of the guys on the team, and what he remembers most about sprinting is how it made him feel. When he started hitting on all cylinders, he felt like he was flying. It didn't feel like his feet were even pushing off the track. It was a euphoric feeling that he has not matched since high school.

Jim's story ...

For some odd reason, around my sixtieth birthday, I decided to sprint one hundred yards on our high school's football field. I just wanted to see what it would be like—see if I could still do it. I've always been an avid hiker and resistance trainer, but I hadn't run, let alone sprinted, in decades. To my surprise, I didn't strain anything and it felt pretty good. I did notice a lot of constriction, though. I tried to will my body to run faster, but it wasn't responding.

I enjoyed the experience, and although my legs did some talking to me the next day, it was a good sore. I decided that each week, I'd do a few sprints at our high school. Amazingly, I felt myself getting faster and my mobility returning. I couldn't resist and just had to know how fast I was running, so I purchased a stopwatch and timed myself. I was shocked when I learned how slow I was. If I raced my sixteen-year-old self in a hundred-yard dash, it would be a darned close race if my present self got a twenty-two-yard head start. And yet, I was amazed by how my sprints made me feel. Even though I wasn't setting any records, I felt electrified. Two of my friends, who are about my age, were so impressed that I was sprinting that they decided to come and join me for a session. Whoops—both pulled their hamstrings. This is a demanding activity and certainly not for everyone.

My sprinting excursion has paid massive dividends. I recently joined a Masters track team. We compete with other After-50s in meets. I like my coaches and my teammates, and sprinting has sponsored new relationships. I never would have guessed that when I first waddled a hundred yards on my high school's football field a couple years ago that it would lead to all this. And I've barely mentioned the health benefits to my heart and my mobility. My resting heart rate has dropped significantly, my stride has improved, and my speed has increased. I have suffered some injuries doing this intense form of movement, but it's been worth it.

Start moving more and be open to where it can take you.

AFTER 50s *Life*

Moving means you're alive. It energizes you. You know that plopping on the couch or collapsing into the chair in front of your computer screen—and remaining there for hour after hour—is miserable for your health and longevity. Develop a plan to introduce more movement into your existence. Measure your progress as you move more and more. Once you're on this glorious path, you'll never look back.

RECLAIM MUSCLE

Start looking like the younger version of yourself

A muscle is like a car. If you want it to run well early in the morning, you have to warm it up.
— FLORENCE GRIFFITH JOYNER, AMERICAN TRACK AND FIELD ATHLETE

THE PROBLEM: YOUR MUSCLES ARE GETTING SMALLER AND WEAKER, AND YOU'RE NOT SURE WHAT TO DO ABOUT IT

MUSCLE IS EXPENSIVE. Your body has to expend a lot of effort to produce it and allocate a lot of calories to develop it and then maintain it. When muscle shrinks, bad things happen. Consider an archetypical example: A sedentary sixty-year-old male is five foot ten and weighs two hundred pounds. In college, he was a lean and powerful 190. Now, nearly forty years later, he's comfortable in the fact that he's only ten pounds heavier than he was in college, but he's delusional. He's lost a quarter of his muscle. He has a pronounced belly because he still eats and drinks roughly the same way he did at age twenty when his body was busy allocating vast resources to growing and maintaining that precious muscle.

Now his body has no choice but to store the excess as fat (bodies have evolved to do this to survive catastrophes). His body composition was youthful at age twenty—low body fat and ample supportive and attractive lean muscle. Now at age sixty, he's not so keen to look at himself in the mirror after he emerges from the shower. His body fat has increased, and his muscles have shrunk. When he starts to assemble all these adverse variables, it dawns on him that his current body composition is far from favorable. He wonders what he can do to bring back some of that twenty-something body.

If you're over fifty, you've lost muscle, too, which is a problem worth fixing. Muscle keeps your posture upright and protects you from injury. Building muscle promotes bone density, and having muscle makes you look and feel younger.

Sarcopenia is the age-related progressive loss of muscle mass and strength. This relentless process can diminish half of your muscle mass by age eighty. It often begins by age forty and accelerates significantly by age sixty. Sarcopenia devastates your posture, restricts your range of motion, and transforms you into a stiff, hunched senior who is susceptible to a catastrophic fall. What's more, you'll have far less muscle padding or bone density to survive a fall without injury.

Sadly, most After-50s don't take action. According to the US Bureau of Labor Statistics, only 10 percent of Americans over the age of fifteen lift weights for exercise. Speculate on this data point for Americans over fifty. How about for women over sixty? These populations no doubt bring that number down significantly. We have a massive opportunity to live far more vibrantly in life's Act II, and we After-50s must take action. We need to slow sarcopenia to a crawl and win some muscle back.

THE HACK: RECLAIM YOUR MUSCLE WITH RESISTANCE TRAINING

Half a century ago, athletes were just beginning to embrace resistance training as a way to enhance performance and mitigate injury. Prior to that, even some professional athletes were discouraged from lifting weights because it could make them muscle-bound and less mobile. Unfortunately, these old prejudices linger. Some After-50s don't participate in resistance training because they fear getting too bulky. It's amazing how often we've heard this.

Others are reluctant to get started because resistance training can seem dangerous, intimidating, expensive, time-consuming, complicated, and, perhaps, not something After-50s should do. Resistance training, though, can be safe, encouraging, efficient, and straightforward, and if you do it in the privacy of your home—it's free.

You want to win back some of the muscle that made you look so good in earlier photos of yourself—pictures in which you stood straight, with a broad smile, when you were mobile and active. Resistance training will help you look more like your younger self. It will not, though, turn you into a clone of vintage 1977 Arnold Schwarzenegger. Getting muscular is hard. Bodybuilders train for hours each day—it's their job. Bodybuilders are mostly younger folks with the perfect genetic cocktail to get huge. Neither of us ever had the DNA mixture to pose in a Speedo. Please don't worry about getting muscular; doing so would take a Herculean effort on your part and probably a time machine. Just focus on reclaiming the muscle you've lost. Now that he's in his seventies, Schwarzenegger still looks pretty fit—another advertisement for resistance training.

The potential for you to improve your body composition is high, particularly if you haven't trained or haven't trained for a long time. And if it does nothing else, resistance training will give you a jolt of energy and make you feel decades younger.

The great news about resistance training is that it's a simple process. Subtract all the aesthetic motivations from the equation. By doing this type of activity, you'll preserve and enhance your ability to perform basic movements that are essential for a vibrant life. Since the earliest days of your existence, you have picked things up, pushed things away, pulled things toward yourself, squatted down, and stood back up. When you lose the ability to do these movements well, your quality of life diminishes. Oh, and one more thing, we need to make certain your important core muscles are strengthened as well. We want to keep you standing as tall as possible.

With a couple of training sessions each week adding up to about one hour of effort, you could be doing something wonderful for your body and your spirit. If you're like many, both old and young, you may find the workouts intoxicating and slightly addicting. You will probably then find yourself doing more. If you give resistance training a try and decide that it's not for you, that's fine. To each her own, but please pat yourself on the back for being adventurous.

WHAT YOU CAN DO TOMORROW

- **Consider your limitations.** Most After-50s have limitations. We both have some arthritic joints. We alter or avoid certain exercises out of caution. This is where your physician's advice is crucial. If she tells you not to do barbell squats because of mobility or injury concerns, listen to her. Almost every resistance training movement has alternative ways and assisted ways to perform it. Your doctor should be enthusiastic about you doing some resistance training and will be a good source of information and advice about how to proceed. It's so important, however, not to let your perceived limitations shut you down.

"I used to do pull-ups to build my deltoids and biceps. Around age fifty-five, I developed bursitis in my left shoulder. This didn't stop me from resistance training; I just replaced pull-ups with a couple of yoga poses that don't aggravate my afflicted shoulder. I get the same result without the pain."

As previously mentioned, we both suffer from arthritis. But we both are convinced that resistance training has been beneficial. If you go to the Arthritis Foundation website, you'll find many resources coaching readers on how to start strength training. Perhaps one of your goals is to feel less arthritis pain. Safe and sane resistance training may help. If your doctor greenlights the idea of doing resistance training, please give it a try.

- **Set goals.** Before embarking on your resistance training journey, ask yourself the following: How could strength training improve my life? What would success look like? These are important questions because resistance training requires time and effort. You may set open-ended goals such as to look better, have more energy, and feel less vulnerable to injury, or you may have specific goals like getting off the floor without putting your hands on your knees and pushing down for leverage, or executing thirty air squats without stopping, or performing a pull-up. Setting goals like these is important for direction and motivation but also as a retort when you're asked why you're doing resistance training by inquisitive friends and family.

  ▶ Compose a brief list of what you hope to accomplish with resistance training.

  ▶ Compose a brief narrative that describes how these accomplishments will impact your life.

  After a period of time, you can compare your results to your goals to see if resistance training has been worth it.

- **Choose your equipment and venue.**
  Before you start on any journey, it's essential
  to scout out your options. Start with logis-
  tics. Where will you resistance train? Both
  of us strength train regularly and do it in
  the comfort and privacy of our homes. But
  if you have a gym membership, this gives
  you impressive options. You can also train at
  home but under the direction of a paid fitness app, and working out this way is popular. You could also hire a personal trainer.
  You must decide what type of equipment
  you'll use. You can get a remarkable workout
  with nothing more than your body weight,
  like Olympic gymnasts, who build muscle
  primarily by pushing, pulling, and squatting their body weight. If you have access to
  weight machines or free weights, that's wonderful. These tools give you many options
  for exercises and allow you to change the
  resistance, which is essential as you start to
  get stronger. An alternative is to train with
  a set of resistance bands. These are like
  massive rubber bands, and they're pretty
  amazing. They come in various widths (the
  wider it is, the more resistance). They're

relatively inexpensive and exceptionally easy on the joints. The poster child for this type of training is Tom Brady. What a marvelous longevity ambassador.

- **Explore bonding opportunities.**
Strength training done in isolation is good. Strength training done communally is awesome. We know because we do both. While we love the convenience of dropping into our basements in the morning and busting out a great workout, there's simply nothing like having a lifting buddy or buddies. You can motivate each other. You can compete with each other. You can hold each other accountable. On the days when you really don't want to train, your resistance training posse will pull you out of your chair and make you join them. You'll thank them later.

BUILDING MOMENTUM

Step 1: Try it for thirty days.

Many experts tout the idea of trying something for twenty-one days; we're advocating a bit larger window. Sure, you could do one session or train two or three times over a week, but a better test drive is thirty days. This gives you a great opportunity to see if you notice benefits. It also breeds familiarity with the movements and the routine and will be a long enough trial for the novelty to wear off. If this activity is still resonating with you after a month, we just might have something here.

Step 2: Map out a one-month schedule.

Note the days you plan to strength train; you can write them on paper or use the calendar or notes app on your smartphone. Give yourself a couple of days between sessions. Obviously, if a scheduling interruption comes up, you can miss a day or postpone a day, but try to hang in there with your self-imposed schedule.

Step 3: Create a list of exercise options for each movement.

- Pushing (examples include push-ups, bench presses, and shoulder presses)
- Pulling (examples include curls, pull-ups or chin-ups, and rowing movements)
- Squatting (examples include squatting, lunging, or leg presses on a machine)
- Core (examples include planks and crunches)

The magic about being a contemporary resistance trainer is that information on what to do and how to do it is literally at your fingertips. Extremely reputable websites, like the Mayo Clinic and Harvard Medical School, offer guidelines on how to start a resistance training program. And these are just two examples. If you search "beginning a resistance training program," you'll find a multitude of options. Then get more specific and search for a detailed term like "resistance training pushing." Peruse the sites you find the most reliable. As you investigate, you'll start to discover corroboration. You can do the same with pulling, squatting, and core movements. You can also search, and this is key, "assisted strength training," and you'll be exposed to ways to make exercises like push-ups or air squats more manageable if you struggle to perform them without help. You can also search "resistance training with household items," and you'll be amazed at the potential. Make a list of pushing, pulling, squatting, and core movements you'd like to try.

> *"I like to get well over 150 active minutes in a week. I use my fitness tracker to monitor my weekly active minutes. What has elated me is how much resistance training, particularly with the legs, contributes to cardio fitness. When you move those big muscles against resistance, your heart gets a great workout too."*

Step 4: Plan your week.

We strength train two to three times a week. We incorporate pushing, pulling, squatting, and core exercises. If you ask ten resistance training practitioners the following questions:

- How much resistance should I use?

- How many sets should I do?

- How many reps should I perform with each exercise?

… you may get ten different answers. Please don't get caught up in this vortex. You can get a great workout with any resistance and any sets and reps as long as you challenge yourself. Make the last few reps hard to perform. We offer this prescription that can be found on many reputable websites. It's safe, sane, and easy to follow, and it can certainly be done with just your body weight or in an assisted fashion. Once you get comfortable, you can start experimenting with variation.

We aim for a resistance level that we can perform eight to twelve times for each set. If twelve reps are performed easily, we add resistance to the next workout. If we can't achieve eight reps, then next time, we'll lighten the load. Jim's lifting sessions generally last thirty to forty-five minutes. Mark prefers high-intensity interval training for about twenty minutes. If you're just starting out, you may use your body weight and do more reps till you feel confident and competent. Then you can graduate to more resistance. But the sets and reps recipe we use is not set in stone. You will adjust it too. You'll get bored otherwise. In the strength training community, there are passionate debates about the proper number of sets and reps. Don't get hung up on these debates. The important part is to get stronger.

Step 5: Watch instructional videos.

It's important to research what to do, but it's also important to watch how to execute each movement. This is where YouTube makes a bold appearance. You can search the proper form for any movement you want to incorporate and then watch a short instructional video with a model using expert form. Using the proper form is the way to ensure that you are doing movements safely and that the exercise is effective at getting you stronger. These video resources are plentiful and easy to find. Take your list of exercises and search for video demonstrations on how to perform them correctly, and then practice with just your body weight and make sure the movement feels safe and feels good.

Step 6: Record your efforts.

You can use a cheap spiral notebook or a desktop or mobile app. Write down the date and the list of exercises you plan to do. Next to each exercise, indicate the level of resistance—which could be just your body weight. Record how many reps you achieve in each set. This will help you adjust your progress or regression (yep, this does happen; some days you won't be feeling it) and can also serve to monitor effectiveness. If one month later, you can do more push-ups than when you started, you'll know your strength has increased, and you have objective evidence to prove it.

This exercise selection process dovetails nicely with the earlier idea of recording your workouts. Enter your training space prior to each workout with a plan. Know exactly what lifts you'll perform and what your goal is for each.

Step 7: Monitor your discomfort.

When you ask your body to move in ways it's unaccustomed to moving, it'll probably get sore. But you need to differentiate between good and bad discomfort. When you strain a muscle or hurt a joint, stop training immediately. That's an injury, which is certainly not your intent. Use great form and a sane level of resistance to guard against this. However, when your muscles are starting to burn due to exhaustion near the end of a challenging set, that's magic. You'll grow to crave this sweet burn. You also may experience significant soreness in the days following a workout. Believe us—this is a great experience, too, and it will go away in a few days. It's a wonderful sign of your body evolving to manage new stress. This badge of honor is like a barometric reading indicating a great workout.

Step 8: Evaluate.

At the end of the month, evaluate your experience. Go back and read your goals. Did you meet them or at least make progress? If you did, you built momentum. Subtle dividends from resistance training can be hard to quantify.

This activity is a big-time confidence-builder. When you feel stronger, you feel better about everything. Your clothes fit better, you stand taller and walk with purpose, you smile more, and you start to recognize an old friend in the mirror. Don't fail to notice these hard-to-measure examples of momentum.

REMOVING OBSTACLES

You've navigated through much of this Hack, but you may still be reluctant to take the resistance training plunge. Unfortunately, you're not alone. Not enough After-50s engage in working their muscles this way. Perhaps these perceived obstacles will resonate with you.

What if I'm too weak to do this? You may be thinking, *This is too much. I can't see myself trying any of this.* We understand. Resistance training can be intimidating. If you fall into this category, here's an idea that could act like a litmus test, and it'll only take a few minutes. Try a farmer's carry. You've done this move a lot. Think of walking with a suitcase in each hand. Find two identical weights that you could carry in each hand. It's important to carry the same amount in each hand for postural integrity. Grab each weight and make sure you're standing straight. Walk around your house, count the number of steps you take until you tire out, and then put the weights down. This can be performed with identical dumbbells, kettlebells, or household items like two gallons of milk or two half-gallons. This exercise will challenge your whole body and improve your grip strength—a key longevity barometer. Try this a few times this week. Were you able to take a few more steps each time you tried? We hope the answer is yes. If you can do it with the farmer's carry, you can do it with all resistance training moves. That's the momentum we want you to embrace.

What if I can't afford resistance training equipment? You don't have to join a gym. You don't have to buy any equipment. If you decide to invest later, you can buy a set of dumbbells (even used ones) or resistance bands. Both options are relatively inexpensive. But understand that you can accomplish tremendous results by using your body weight. Numerous examples exist of individuals in captivity (think Nelson Mandela and Joseph Pilates) who thrived physically using the weight of their own bodies. If your body is too heavy, you can alter movements and use doorways, counters, and furniture to assist you. You can also use household items and inexpensive resistance bands to greatly ramp up the intensity.

Please don't let this perceived obstacle deter you. Some of the fittest athletes in the world do not use anything but the weight of their own bodies to train.

What if I hurt myself? Both of us suffer from arthritis. Most medical professionals agree that strength training is good for just about everyone, and it's especially impactful for those suffering from arthritis. A wonderful way to stay safe is to strive to use great form with every movement and to select an appropriate amount of resistance. Immediately stop if you strain a muscle. If this happens, don't return to the exercise until your strained muscle feels normal. Like any physical activity, injuries can occur. The great news is that none of us needs to play hurt in the big game this Sunday. Just relax and give yourself time to heal before you return to the lift. You can also train with non-injured muscle groups while you're waiting for your affected area to recuperate. And remember the directives on discomfort management in the previous section.

THE HACK IN ACTION

Jim has never been a very big guy. In fact, he's heard himself described as slightly built. He's carried 150 pounds around, sometimes a bit more, sometimes a bit less, his whole adult life. Some may look at this homeostasis as enviable, but that's a limited perspective. Jim comes from slight ancestors. Arthritis afflicted these earlier relatives just like it afflicts him. He keeps his joints healthy and functioning through resistance training.

When Jim was in college, he became obsessed with weightlifting. At the time, he viewed it as a way to pack on badly needed muscle. He was amazed at how well it worked.

Jim's story ...

I think back to the younger me in the weight room and just close my eyes and smile. My energy level was unbounded. I couldn't wait to get out of class and rush to work out. My body transformed during my freshman year. My legs became more powerful, my pectoral muscles became more pronounced, and my biceps and triceps became defined. I loved the feeling of the workout. The blood rushing to your muscles in the last few reps of a set is an epic feeling of power and potential. I got a lot stronger. I started to draw the attention of many of the really big guys who worked out there. They started to encourage me, and I developed some lifelong friends. I felt more confident as I walked the campus.

After graduation, I began teaching high school social studies. I also coached football, and my fellow coaches were impressed with my knowledge of strength training. So was the school administration. I became the school's first paid strength and conditioning coach. I coached many activities, like football, track and field, and mock trial, but teaching kids how to strength train was my favorite. My fondest memory from this tenure was when I was twenty-seven. The kids cheered me on as I achieved my lifelong dream of bench pressing three hundred pounds, which was twice my body weight.

Now, I'm in my sixties. I still teach as an adjunct in the education department at a local university. You better believe that after class a few days each week, I hustle over to the fitness center and bust out a workout with the students. It's always a sentimental experience to watch these young men and women enthusiastically pump out reps.

Many of them are impressively strong, but they welcome my presence. They encourage me every time I show up. And it's not just the students in the weight room. My wife loves that I still strength train. Sometimes, she'll even throw a flirty compliment my way. She strength trains, too, and looks fantastic. When I don't work out at school, we work out together, which is a wonderful bonding experience. I see a general practitioner and a cardiologist each year. Both medical professionals are fully on board with my resistance training regimen. They've echoed all the ideas we've shared in this Hack—it's great for increasing bone density, improving balance, reducing arthritis, boosting cardio fitness, and developing an overall sense of well-being.

I can't bench three hundred pounds anymore, but using an online max estimation calculator, I'm closing in on two hundred, which would be quite an achievement for an "old guy." I'm as excited about meeting this more modest goal as I was at my peak strength. What's more, I still feel that same euphoric pump.

AFTER 50s Life

Resistance training can reverse the effects of aging. We cannot think of a stronger endorsement. This Hack is all about reclaiming some of that valuable lost muscle. It bears repeating that the goal is not to make you look like a bodybuilder but to reclaim some of the muscle that Father Time has stolen. Resistance training has the potential to make you more recognizable when you look in the mirror.

PART 3

MENTAL AND EMOTIONAL WELL-BEING

NURTURE

Pause, breathe, and get some sun

*Meditation is all about the pursuit of nothingness.
It's like the ultimate rest. It's better than the best
sleep you've ever had. It's a quieting of the mind. It
sharpens everything, especially your appreciation
of your surroundings. It keeps life fresh.*
— HUGH JACKMAN, AUSTRALIAN ACTOR

THE PROBLEM: IT'S EASY TO IGNORE
MENTAL AND EMOTIONAL HEALTH

WE EQUATE THE spirit to the soul—something in each
of us that is not physical or material—the part that
leads people to kindness, empathy, and love. The mind and
soul must, we believe, be nurtured. They need care, encouragement, and growth. They require momentum, even for
people well into life's Act II—perhaps even more for them.

Unfortunately, it's easy to ignore what we can't see. In prior Hacks, we've provided ideas and strategies about tangible things: how to approach life's Act II (you can see the end of a career), how to take care of your body (you can see a growing waistline), and how to maintain healthy muscles and joints (you can feel an aching back). We can't see the mind and soul, though, making it easy to race through our often-chaotic days, never pausing for even a few brief moments to nurture these important parts of our total being.

Additionally, as we age, much like the physical body, our mind and soul succumb more to feeling down with the strain of life. Career moves, impending retirement, parenting, relationships, and grief add to daily stress, which we know is debilitating in so many ways. Throw in unforeseen issues like a pandemic, political upheaval, and increasing natural disasters, and our emotional health becomes even more endangered. After-50s watch once-vibrant parents grow old, tired, and in too many cases, sick and cognitively impaired. The end of life sometimes can be harder on friends and family than it is on mentally debilitated people, living what often appears to be a poor quality of life. We've seen this firsthand; it's extremely challenging to watch and wait for someone to die to get relief from their pain. And that challenge doesn't end when the loved one passes away. It's easy to pine away, failing to continue the momentum we've discussed. Researchers, including Jonathan Rauch, author of *The Happiness Curve*, have identified a midlife malaise, depression, or a dip in happiness, largely due to a variety of the problems we've identified.

The good news is that you can mitigate this malaise and be happier than you once were with a few simple strategies.

THE HACK: PAUSE, BREATHE, AND GET SOME SUN

The beauty of this Hack is that while it does contain a few strategies we haven't covered, it also includes a combination of earlier Hacks, which we're guessing you've already tried or may have been doing prior to reading this book. Nurturing the mind and soul begins with nurturing the body. Believe it or not, there's plenty of indisputable science that connects a healthy, mostly plant-based, diet to improved mental and emotional health. In Hack 3, we discussed the impact of creating your own balanced diet—one that leads to health and happiness while giving you an edge in your battle with Father Time. Turns out, your new way of eating will also lead to better sleep (we cover this in Hack 7) and more energy, and these put you on a path to feeling good about yourself.

Hack 4 (movement) and Hack 5 (resistance training) focused on maintaining a strong, flexible body. You guessed it: movement and exercise also improve your mental well-being. Studies by the Mayo Clinic list numerous psychological benefits of exercise, including releasing endorphins, escaping worries, and building confidence—all keys to nurturing your mind and soul. While movement and restorative sleep do wonders for your mental health, when you combine these with meditation, mindfulness, deep breathing, and sunshine, your chances of fighting off mental disorders and increasing happiness are likely to increase exponentially.

WHAT YOU CAN DO TOMORROW

- **Meditate.** While it is thousands of years old, meditation has become more popular in recent years. It is a strategy widely recommended by mental health practitioners to help people relax during times of stress and to invigorate the body and the mind while providing clarity of thought and increased energy. Even if you have previously dismissed meditation as silly, a waste of time, or an activity that's just not for you, we want you to give it a try. Many books, articles, and videos can show you how to get started. We'll save you some time and provide a few surprisingly simple steps you can do at this moment (read all of them, then set the book aside and dive in):

  ▸ Find a quiet place.

  ▸ Sit in an upright position (lying down can work, but it increases the risk of falling asleep). Contrary to what you may have seen in pictures or on TV, your legs do not need to be crossed in any particular way.

▸ Close your eyes.

▸ Inhale deeply through your nose.

▸ Exhale slowly.

▸ Focus only on your breathing (it may help to silently count the breaths). When a stray thought enters your mind, push it aside and return your focus to the breath.

▸ Start with about ten breaths or one minute of meditation (using a timer can help keep you focused).

▸ Smile and congratulate yourself for being intentional about your mental and emotional well-being.

"If you struggle with the idea of meditating–you are not alone. What I have come to learn is that your meditation may look different from what people picture. Last winter, I became obsessed with doing a daily five-minute cold plunge in 48-degree water (this was the temperature of my tap water last January if I adjusted it to cold). I did this for one month and calmed my desire to get the heck out of that tub by focusing my mind and calming my breaths. By the end of the month, I was doing my plunge with no sweat (pun intended). That, my friend, is meditation!"

- **Breathe.** We hear you. Of course, you're already breathing. Plus, if you follow our simple meditation steps, they include a routine breathing exercise. We want you to try diaphragmatic breathing, also known as belly breathing. The diaphragm is a large muscle located at the base of your lungs. Diaphragmatic breathing enhances lung capacity, which helps you exercise more efficiently, reduce blood pressure, and relax. The latter benefit of belly breathing, of course, plays a crucial role in nurturing your mind and soul. And yes, you can do it right now by following these steps:

  ‣ Lie down in a comfortable spot.

  ‣ Raise your knees or place a pillow beneath them.

  ‣ Place one hand on your chest and one on your stomach below the ribs.

  ‣ Breathe in slowly through your nose (your stomach should rise beneath your hand).

  ‣ Breathe out through pursed lips, making a swooshing sound.

  ‣ Repeat the cycle five to ten times.

- **Be mindful.** Similar to meditation, mindfulness is a calming activity that focuses the mind. Unlike meditation, though, mindfulness is less about focusing on breathing and more about focusing on a single thing. Mindfulness can be done with the eyes opened or closed. When you are practicing mindfulness, you find one idea on which to focus your thoughts and senses, and you fully attend to what is happening in that moment. For example, you might start your morning with a cup of coffee or tea at the kitchen table or on your patio. To make this a mindful moment, focus your attention completely on your beverage, pushing your mind away from all other distractions— a newspaper, a mobile device, upcoming events, and even people. Any thoughts should be about the experience of drinking that coffee or tea: the smell of the liquid, any steam rising from it, the saliva gathering in anticipation of it, the texture of the liquid in your mouth, and the feel of the cup in your hands and on your fingers. Because you can be mindful about anything, as with the prior strategies, you can also try mindfulness at this very moment.

- **Get some sun (or at least some natural light).** Remember John Denver's popular song "Sunshine on My Shoulders"? Like the late singer, we're big believers in the power of sunshine. Denver, of course, was not a doctor. Still, we challenge you to find lyrics that provide a more accurate or impactful theme for healthy living (we also dare you to try not to hum that tune for the rest of the day). Sunshine increases the release of serotonin, which can improve your mood and make you feel more focused. There is an almost magical quality to sunshine and natural light. Even if it's cloudy, getting outside for ten minutes of light can ignite a spark in your soul. And, dare we revisit the theme of this section, you can do it right now unless you're reading this at nighttime.

BUILDING MOMENTUM

In The Problem section at the beginning of this Hack, we noted that it's easy to ignore mental health; many people simply don't think much about their mind and their soul. We've provided simple, practical steps to overcome this problem. Now, we need to turn those try-it-now steps into long-term self-care habits. Here's how to do it:

Step 1: Focus on nutrition.

Think about foods that increase fatigue and lower your mood:

- processed meats
- fried food
- most cereals
- high-fat dairy products

Your meal planner (you, if you're adhering to our earlier Hack and mastering meal planning) should eliminate most of these; of course, with balance in mind, you can mix in one or two servings periodically. Replace these in your daily meal plan with mood enhancers:

- whole grains
- fruits
- vegetables
- fish
- nuts

These will provide the energy and clarity to inspire you to move frequently throughout your day.

Step 2: Make deep breathing and meditation daily routines.

You may have already set this book aside and given diaphragmatic breathing and meditation a quick, one-minute test run. We're guessing you instantly felt better. The key to mental and emotional well-being, though, is to turn these quick mood enhancers into habits. One way to do both deep breathing and meditation every day is via habit stacking (credit to *Atomic Habits* author James Clear for this one). We all have daily habits that are ingrained in our routines. To make a simple meditation or deep-breathing practice a habit, try coupling, or stacking, it with one of your always-do habits. Think of something you do automatically each day, then consider adding a few minutes of meditation or deep breathing to that habit.

"I like to listen to audiobooks or music when I walk throughout the day. During my morning walk, though, I leave my earbuds at home, and I focus on mindfulness. With no extra distractions, I practice being mindful of nature. I think about the health benefits of the sun, and I listen intently to the birds chirping or the tree branches fluttering against the breeze. I smile, acknowledging the beauty around me, and I feel great heading into the rest of my day."

Step 3: Leverage technology.

We are big believers in modern technology and leveraging its power to make us better human beings. Jim has written widely about using tech to improve teaching and learning in his *Hacking Engagement* books, and Mark considers himself an early adopter (not to the point of standing in line for the newest smartphone, mind you). We do like to remain agnostic when it comes to brands, though. Regardless of the kind of device or app market you prefer, you can download a meditation app today if you don't already have one. Some of the wearable fitness devices come with apps that include meditation and breathing guides. You'll find dozens of free meditation apps in the market that can help you get started and maintain a meditation, mindfulness, and breathing routine. Combine your app with smartphone reminders to meditate or breathe, and you make this important part of nurturing your mind and soul surprisingly easy.

Step 4: Commune with nature.

Based on some fairly nonscientific research, Finland is considered to be the happiest place in the world. In a 2021 survey by Finnish research company Sitra, Finns shared what makes them happy, and 87 percent of the population rated nature as either very or fairly important (you can read about this study at sitra.fi). Even more notable than most Finns' belief in the impact of nature on happiness, 65 percent of survey respondents said they believe nature gives them peace of mind. We couldn't agree more. Apart from the health benefits of sunshine mentioned earlier, getting outside encourages movement (another critical contributor to mental health), and it brings us closer to flora and fauna, which can spark an appreciation for the vibrant life around us. We find that when we appreciate this vibrancy, it feeds our Momentum Mindset, which contributes to health and longevity. The key to communing with nature is similar to the strategies for routine meditation and deep breathing: combine these activities until they turn into habits. For example, you can do deep breathing while walking in the sunshine (keep your eyes open in this case). You can take your coffee or tea outside and enjoy your mindful moment while listening to the birds chirp. Better still, you can play a round of golf, go for a hike in the woods, or play a game of pickleball outside; now, you're nurturing your mind and soul while moving and creating resistance for your muscles. This is the best of all worlds.

OVERCOMING OBSTACLES

Many ideas and strategies in this Hack may be completely foreign to you. At the risk of stereotyping, we know many After-50s who think meditation, communing with nature, and other mental health practices are nonsensical ideas endorsed by fad science and hucksters looking to sell supplements, online courses, or books (the irony of the latter is palpable). The stigma around mental well-being creates doubt that can make the simple solutions we provide in this Hack difficult to accept. Please consider our responses to these issues we face from doubters.

Many physicians do not recommend any of this. Keep in mind that your general care doctor, holistic practitioner, or geriatrician may not specialize in matters of the mind and the soul. Even many psychiatrists prefer to prescribe medicines for anxiety and depression rather than encourage people with these disorders to focus on natural strategies. (Quick reminder: we are not doctors and have no licenses or certifications around mental health or psychological well-being; if you are troubled by any mental disorder, please see a doctor.) This does not mean that a large portion of the ever-evolving medical community is not on board with these ideas and strategies. You can find many impactful books, videos, and podcasts produced by licensed medical professionals proclaiming the profound physical and mental impact of meditation, deep breathing, sunshine, and a mostly plant-based diet.

I've tried meditation, but my mind just wanders too much. Even the most skilled practitioners of meditation struggle to calm the mind and quell disruptive thoughts. Some meditation instructors tell students to think of nothing. We'd argue that this is impossible. In *Meditation for Beginners*, Vern Lovic refers to the flood of thoughts that some beginners call a wandering mind as "the circus." Rather than eliminate it, Lovic suggests focusing on the breath as much as possible and trying to stretch the time that you do not notice anything except your breath. The key is to acknowledge these intermittent interruptions of your meditation. Say to yourself, *That was a stray thought that interrupted my focus; I'm going to push it aside and return to the breath.* This is fine, and random thoughts are a normal part of meditation. Don't allow these brief interruptions to steer you away from this wonderful practice.

This is too time-consuming. In Hack 4, we encourage plenty of daily movement, which can indeed add years to your life. One beauty of this book, we think and hope you agree, is how combining various strategies not only helps you live a long, joy-filled life, but it also saves you time. As noted earlier in this Hack, you can combine walking and mindfulness. You can couple deep breathing with meditation (count your breaths to ward off intrusive thoughts). Play some tennis, toss a ball around with a friend or grandchild, or spend fifteen minutes in the garden, and you get the benefit of movement while soaking up some sun. With the goal of living a fabulous After-50s life, you can certainly find the time to nurture your mind and soul.

THE HACK IN ACTION

Mark's story …

After teaching in the 7–12 classroom for twenty-three years, I decided to resign in 2013 to pursue consulting opportunities. This was a life-impacting decision that came with a high level of risk. In addition to leaving the comfort of my decades-long routine of driving a short distance from home to school daily, working with longtime friends and colleagues, and teaching in the district where my wife also taught, I was suddenly thrust into a life of travel. Not only am I a nervous traveler by nature, but this new profession kept me away from home and from my spouse and two young children. It didn't take long before my anxiety and blood pressure shot up. I needed help.

A friend recommended meditation, and I tried it about six months after my career change. As a novice practitioner, I struggled with a wandering mind (we address this in the Overcoming Obstacles section of this Hack). After a few months, I gave up on meditation. During the next few years as my career path continued to zigzag, my struggles with anxiety and what I believe to be an undiagnosed mildly depressive state continued. Making matters worse, I was in what seemed like a constant state of physical flux as I tried numerous medications to treat the epilepsy I had been diagnosed with over a decade earlier. I managed to work and write a bit while trying to be a good husband and father. Still, I wasn't always happy. Too often, I was frustrated and sad.

A few years removed from the classroom and after entering the After-50s phase of life, I decided to get serious about health, fitness, and mental well-being. While this book is not bogged down with a ton of references, Jim's and my experience always starts with research, and this is where I began my pursuit of mental and emotional well-being.

I turned to many experts in the field—Peter Attia, Jason Fung, Robert Waldinger, Tony Robbins, Vern Lovic, David A. Sinclair, Sharon Stone (yes, the movie star), Dan Buettner, and Tom Brady (yes, the football star), to name just a few. Some of these luminaries are medical doctors, some are researchers, and some are, like me, practitioners. All of these, and many experts I've studied who are not mentioned here, have experience in physical fitness, mental health, or overcoming obstacles. I was entering Act II of my life, hoping for five or six more decades yet struggling with anxiety and disease, and I needed something. Books, articles, and podcasts by the people I've listed helped me learn how to nurture my mind and my soul.

Encouraged by James Clear's habit stacking concept, I adapted my own stacking plan. This involved working with ideas and strategies from one expert, adapting them to my needs, and combining them with other ideas I'd learned elsewhere. (This is the essence of Hack Learning—seeing problems through a unique lens and adapting existing information and solutions to create something new.) So, I designed my own mental and emotional well-being plan, including a healthy diet, exercise, getting outside more than ever, meditation, mindfulness, and diaphragmatic breathing. My quality of life as I approach sixty and in spite of numerous stressful situations—grief from the loss of friends and both parents and ongoing battles with epilepsy and long COVID—is better than ever. Each day begins with a clear mind and a full heart. And while every day is not perfect, there's always some joy.

We believe that living a long, healthy, joy-filled life requires an amalgam of the strategies in this book. You can feed your body all the best vitamins and minerals, sleep like a baby nightly, and pump iron alongside world-class bodybuilders at the gym. Any of these will give you a leg up on Father Time. If you want it all, though—physical health, joy, and longevity—you need to nurture your mind and your soul. With the strategies in this Hack, you can start today.

RECHARGE

Create a restorative routine and sleep your way to a longer life

Asleep, he looked a lot younger than going-on-seventeen, but I had noticed that Johnny looked younger when he was asleep too, so I figured everyone did. Maybe people are younger when they are asleep.
— S.E. HINTON, AUTHOR OF THE OUTSIDERS

THE PROBLEM: SLEEP IS UNDERRATED

POPULAR ACTOR SAM Elliott played tough guy Wade Garrett in the late '80s cult film *Roadhouse*. When asked if he ever slept, Elliott's character deadpanned, "I'll get all the sleep I need when I'm dead." Garrett would soon learn if his quip was correct, as the town thugs ended his life a few days later. *Roadhouse*'s thin plot may not be relevant here; Wade

Garrett's feelings on sleep, though, are worth exploring. Many people believe, as Elliott's fictional character did, that living life to the fullest means sacrificing shuteye for late nights of dancing, drinking, and debauchery. While we may not be experts at whatever late-night activities bring you joy, we do know a few things about the impact of restorative sleep on health and longevity.

It's not shocking that most people underestimate the value of sleep. The medical profession waited until the early twentieth century to launch the first sleep lab and study the effects of chronic sleep deprivation, and psychological studies of insomnia didn't take hold until the 1970s. Now, in the twenty-first century, we still don't fully understand sleep, but we do know that not getting enough of it has many deleterious effects on one's physical and mental well-being. Studies by the Cleveland Clinic and the National Sleep Foundation identify many issues caused by lack of sleep. Short-term problems include a lack of focus, impaired memory, and a reluctance to exercise due to added fatigue. Long-term issues include high blood pressure, diabetes, depression, a lower sex drive, dementia, and even heart failure or stroke. As noted earlier, the Standard American Diet is a killer. Its biggest ally may be insomnia or simply a lack of good sleep.

While it's easy to ignore sleep, especially for young people who recover more quickly from late nights, it can be quite challenging to follow a routine that leads to the seven to nine hours of good sleep that After-50s need. The rigors of work, parenthood, grandparenthood, community activities, late-night TV, and other pursuits can all factor into restlessness, intermittent sleep, and even insomnia.

Poor sleep hygiene (yes, this really is a thing) also interferes with your body's ability to reboot. While you're likely familiar with bad sleep hygiene, it's worth mentioning a few of the biggest contributors to non-restorative sleep. High-fat and high-sugar diets, late-night dinners, alcohol consumption close to bedtime, heavy evening exercise, long naps, and blue light from mobile devices are a few sleep inhibitors. There are others, though, that you may not consider. While late-night exercise is risky, not exercising at all may be more impactful on how well you sleep; lack of movement throughout the day can lead to nighttime energy or agitation. In short, everything you do during the day impacts how well you sleep at night, and most people don't take sound sleep seriously, which is a huge blockade on the road to health and longevity.

THE HACK: CREATE AND PRACTICE A RESTORATIVE ROUTINE

Throughout this book, we discuss the positive impact of a proper diet, movement, and a Momentum Mindset on your general well-being and longevity. It is possible, though, that nothing plays a bigger role in long-term physical and mental health than consistent nights of peaceful, restorative sleep. You may know people who claim to function just fine on four to six hours of slumber. By and large, After-50s need seven to nine hours of restful sleep, including the requisite amount of light, deep, and REM sleep. Please note that we're talking about actual sleep—not the hours you spend in your bed. But how does one consistently get this seemingly insane amount of sleep?

"I once loved to boast that I got eight hours of sleep–in bed at ten, up at six. When I started tracking my sleep with wearable technology and the accompanying mobile app, I realized I was awake for much of that time and was often missing out on much-needed REM and deep sleep."

The strategy (create a restorative routine) is easy; the execution, though, can present a challenge. Here's how to get started.

WHAT YOU CAN DO TOMORROW

- **Plan your entire day around sleep.**
  When you get out of bed, start thinking ahead to when you'll return—fourteen to sixteen hours later. Consider a few practices that will improve your sleep:
    ▸ Consuming the right foods throughout the day. Choose mostly low-fat, low-sugar foods, which play an important role in the amount of deep sleep you

get nightly (refer to Hack 3 about meal planning).

- ▸ Exercise to burn energy. Remember Hack 4? The more you move, the better your body and brain will be. Plus, your tired body will alert your brain that it's time to sleep, or vice-versa.

- ▸ Think about sleeping well. Train your brain to focus on good sleep, especially if you typically don't think about it.

- **Start a sleep routine.** This is not a novel strategy; you may have read about sleep hygiene. Still, if you're as serious about sleep as you should be, it's time to start a routine of your own. Consider any of these impactful steps, and commit to at least one today:

  - ▸ Settle on a one-hour sleep window: think about when you're typically sleepy, and plan to go to bed each night sometime in that sixty-minute window.

  - ▸ Reflect on what you do daily within two hours of your sleep window and try to eliminate activities that corrupt restorative sleep: vigorous exercise, heavy meals, sugary snacks, stress, a lot of alcohol, and blue light from screens.

- ▸ Eat your heavy meals at breakfast or lunch; light dinners influence better sleep.
- ▸ Take a hot shower, bath, or sauna an hour or two before sleep. There's sound research backing the impact of warming up the body before bed.
- ▸ Meditate in the hour or two before sleep. Tons of free mobile apps can help you wind down in the evening.

- **Identify your biggest sleep deterrent.** Many insomniacs have no idea why they don't sleep, and, sadly, some are given poor advice by doctors who are not sleep experts. Mark was labeled an insomniac for many years by a physician whose best advice was to take melatonin (new research refutes the positive impact of this practice). When he got serious about his health and well-being, Mark learned that better habits throughout the day were the most important factors to restorative sleep. What was his biggest deterrent? Too much caffeine close to bedtime.

- **Turn off or move your bedroom television.** Watching TV in bed is a surefire way to toss and turn throughout the night. Studies reveal that the negative impacts of the blue light radiating from your TV or other screens are plentiful. Want to start sleeping soundly tonight? Turn off the bedroom TV or move it to another room (this goes double for your mobile devices).

BUILDING MOMENTUM

When you try one or several sleep strategies outlined in the prior section, you should see an immediate improvement in your sleep. The goal is to get to that magic range of seven to nine hours of consistent, restorative sleep (let's say, at least five nights a week). The following steps will get you there quickly.

Step 1: Be intentional about your routine.

If you commit to a sleep window starting at 10–11 p.m., start planning to meet this commitment at 7–8 p.m. If you're dining out, set your reservation for 6 p.m. or sooner. Not only is eating several hours before bedtime important for your metabolism, but it also provides plenty of time for you to get back home and prepare for sleep. Once you've decided what habits work best for you—a hot bath, meditation, a leisurely post-dinner walk—follow through with them nightly (mixing up these pre-sleep routines should make managing your routine easy).

One of the toughest parts of this practice is interference from other people. While it's fine to break from routine once or twice a week, maybe staying up late to gather with friends, it's important to fight the urge to depart from your habits too often.

Pro Tip: Make your friends and loved ones part of your support team. Explain your effort to improve sleep; maybe even explain your new routine. And, most important, tell them you need their support. Our guess is they'll love your commitment to a better life and be all in on helping you live it.

Step 2: Combine a few Hacks.

Remember, this isn't just about sleep hygiene. To make a substantial change in sleep—maybe even lose that "insomniac" label—you need more than a few nighttime habits. Revisit Hacks 5, 4, and 3 on resistance training, movement, and diet, respectively. These all play major roles in restorative sleep. Use the strategies in those Hacks throughout each day and combine them with what you've learned in this Hack, and soon, nightly blissful slumber will become part of your happiness and well-being system. This is the Momentum Mindset we've alluded to throughout this book. Use one or two strategies, and you'll certainly improve. Combine most or all strategies into your own personalized system, and you'll move toward a long, healthy, joy-filled life.

Step 3: Reimagine your bedroom.

We know it sounds like a commercial for a home remodeling company, and you've likely heard it before. Where you sleep, though, can have as much impact on how you sleep as most of the other factors we've discussed in this Hack. In a prior section, we recommended shutting off or removing all screens from your bedroom. In addition to this important strategy, you can also apply as many of these as possible:

- Lower the temperature. As people age, they tend to feel colder than when they were younger. They layer clothing and turn up the heat. For sleep, though, set your room temp at sixty-five or lower. Science says we sleep better in cold rooms. Don't worry; it's okay to get under the covers if you begin to shiver.

- Go dark. The brain tells the body it's time to sleep when it's dark. This is part of the body's circadian rhythm—physical and mental changes that occur during a twenty-four-hour cycle. While some people prefer to leave blinds open or turn on a night light, it's best to make your bedroom as dark as possible. As noted earlier, Mark used to be an insomniac, and along with other poor habits, he liked a little light in the room. When he got serious about sleep, it was curtains closed and lights turned off.

"My wife convinced me to start wearing a sleep mask. Picture one of those eye masks you see on the faces of pampered TV divas. I wear one of those. I've grown to enjoy the mild pressure on my face, and it blocks out all light. I'm hooked!"

- Invest in comfort. One of the best gifts you can give yourself is a state-of-the-art mattress and a cooling pillow. Non-cooling pillows maintain body heat, and a hot head (no pun intended) can keep you awake.

   Pro Tip: Spend an hour or two at your local mattress store and try out a few beds and pillows; the salespeople don't mind.

- Consider sleeping alone. This strategy is unique to those who sleep with someone who may disrupt their slumber with excessive flip-flopping or snoring. As emphasized throughout this Hack, impactful, restorative sleep is far too important to ignore, even if it means giving your significant other the boot. We're not advocating celibacy. You can still be intimate in your bedroom; when it's time to sleep, though, you or your disruptive partner must go.

Step 4: Nap responsibly.

You've heard many people rave about their wonderful midday naps. Some pro athletes even embrace a daily snooze. If your brief respite is truly a catnap—fifteen minutes or less—and you nap infrequently, you needn't worry. However, studies by the American Heart Association indicate that daily naps and long naps can have serious health implications, including an increased risk of diabetes and cardiovascular disease. Be dedicated to getting seven to nine hours of outstanding sleep, and naps will soon be obsolete.

Step 5: Track your sleep.

Wearable fitness technology is growing in popularity, and many such devices are integrating sophisticated sleep-tracking features. Several mattress brands also incorporate technology that can monitor sleep and provide data on an accompanying app. We discuss the power of tech throughout this book. Remember, you can only precisely know how well you sleep when you track the time you're sleeping versus the time you're awake. Plus, good technology will show you your nightly sleep score; how much light, REM, and deep sleep you're getting; and how often you're restless. This information is invaluable. The image at the beginning of this chapter shows an example of Mark's sleep score one night.

REMOVING OBSTACLES

According to the Sleep Foundation, more than 35 percent of adults in the US report sleeping less than seven hours a night. Roughly 40 percent of insomniacs have some type of mental disorder. The Foundation's research reveals many more staggering sleep-related statistics and problems. Still, as adults around the world become increasingly aware of the importance of sleep, many continue to neglect the issue. Here are a few common obstacles related to improving sleep and how to overcome them.

Going to bed before 11 p.m. or midnight is unreasonable. We'd all love more time in our days. If you find yourself working or playing late into the night, budgeting your time may be a problem worthy of an entire new Hack. Meanwhile, we recommend focusing on an earlier strategy: being intentional about your routine. This may include sacrifices, such as carving out different times for work or cutting back on some leisure activities (TV and social media are great places to start). Regardless of how you do it, focus on a routine that makes time for sleep. Start by reminding yourself that more sleep may help you live longer, and this is certainly time worth earning.

Trading yummy food for good sleep isn't fun. Remember, your diet is only one part of an entire lifestyle that leads to impactful, restorative sleep. Consuming heavy meals, especially late-night dinners, can increase the time it takes to fall asleep and interfere with restful sleep.

You'll enjoy that high-carb meal or sugary snack only for a short time; the residuals from the extra good sleep will last well into the following day, and feeling energized in the morning is definitely more fun.

Falling asleep without television feels impossible. Have you tried it? Most people who sleep with a TV started at a young age or married someone who is used to bedroom TV. Before you break out the tools and remove your wall-mounted boob tube, start by shutting it off for just one night; in fact, don't even turn it on. Instead, try reading, doing some light stretching, or, if you sleep with a partner, having sex—a proven way to reduce stress and unwind for sleep. Try these and other relaxing bedroom activities for a few nights, and before you know it, you won't even consider TV in bed.

What if I've been napping for years? The Momentum Mindset is about forward motion, along with balance. First, focus on the positive impact of change. Second, start small. If you nap every day, cut one day. When you feel sleepy, replace the nap with a brisk walk, a few yoga poses, or a short drive to a store. The activity will quickly eliminate the lethargy. A day or two later, try it again. Listen to your body and do what's right for your needs. Balance and momentum are the keys to success.

All this focus on sleep could be counterproductive. This is a legitimate concern. When you're determined to improve something, you can overdo it. If you find yourself becoming too invested in your fitness tracker sleep score each morning, or if you avoid important social opportunities with friends and family because you don't want to disrupt your sleep schedule, or even worse, if you begin to consider yourself a failure when you have a bout of insomnia, it's time to pull in the reins. A good night's sleep is important, but you don't want to exhaust yourself trying to obtain it. This obstacle can be a real issue for our high-achieving readers. Please take the right steps, and if you have a bad night, try again the next night.

THE HACK IN ACTION

Mark's story ...

For much of my life's Act I, I was a terrible sleeper. Most nights, I slept fewer than seven hours, and nights of uninterrupted sleep were few and far between. For decades, I wore this affliction like a badge of honor, as if sleeping poorly exemplified some kind of fortitude or toughness. "I slept terribly last night," I'd announce to friends or colleagues. "No problem; I'll fight through the fatigue and get everything done." Sometimes, I'd declare that I didn't need a lot of sleep. What I failed to realize was just how much my insomnia impacted my productivity and my mood.

On many occasions, I wasn't sharp. My mental focus was blurry, and the mounting fatigue often made me end my workdays early or, worse, led to poor productivity and sloppy performance. While I often failed to notice when I wasn't getting enough sleep, I was unhappy and sometimes downright irritable. As I got older and started seeing my physician regularly (as we've recommended in various spots throughout this book), she added the word "insomniac" to my chart. This was always a discussion point at annual physical exams, and the advice was usually the same: drink less alcohol, exercise more, and take melatonin. I tried melatonin, which did not alleviate my restless nights and served only to make me groggy in the mornings. While I stopped using insomnia as a badge of honor, I accepted the fact that I would likely live out my life as a bad sleeper.

THE TURNING POINT

In Hack 3, I shared my battle with long COVID and how it led to a significant change in my diet. Changing how I eat was mainly about eating less of what causes inflammation, fatigue, and other physical problems I wanted to overcome. An added benefit was how eating the right foods impacted sleep. In the early stages of my COVID struggles, I purchased an Oura Ring—a fitness-tracking device similar to the popular watches that track activity, sleep quality, heart rate, and other aspects of general well-being. We remain technology agnostic, and this is not a promotion for one device (while Oura works for me, Fitbit or another brand may work well for you). We are believers in using modern technology to track fitness.

The mobile app that connects to my ring keeps me informed about my nightly sleep quality. It also comes with a tagging feature, which you can use to identify variables that may impact sleep. For example, on rare occasions when I have a late dinner heavy in refined carbohydrates and sugars, I can note this on my app. If I go to bed significantly later than usual, the app tracks this. Over time, I can review how well I slept and use these variables to learn the factors that most impact my sleep. It only took about two months of tracking my sleep before I realized the strategies in this Hack not only help me sleep better than ever before, but they also have cured my insomnia. Please understand that this is a personal observation—not a medical diagnosis.

What I can say unequivocally is that I average seven to eight hours of restorative sleep. And I know, based on the evidence recorded in my Oura app, that the key to consistent, impactful sleep is employing the strategies in this Hack every day. I consume foods that contain the vitamins and nutrients my body needs, I go to bed within the same one-hour window nightly, I exercise daily at times that don't deter sleep, I avoid stress when possible, and I'm intentional about my routine, understanding that high-quality restorative sleep improves my mood and productivity and will, in all likelihood, help me live a long, joy-filled life.

AFTER 50s *Life*

After ignoring the impact of sleep on physical and mental health and longevity for centuries, most doctors, researchers, and longevity experts are now trumpeting the value of nightly restorative sleep. Now, you can easily find medical centers and research labs dedicated solely to the study of sleep, offering sound clinical advice on how to improve your slumber and defeat insomnia. We looked into many of these while conducting our research on sleep. More importantly, we've practiced the strategies these organizations espouse—most of which we've shared in this Hack. We sleep well, and we feel better because of it. We're certain you will too.

PART 4

VITALITY, IMPACT, COMMUNITY

DABBLE

An engaged After-50 is a happy After-50

*You cannot teach a man anything, you can
only help him find it within himself.*
— GALILEO, ASTRONOMER

THE PROBLEM: YOU'RE BORED

LIFE FOR AFTER-50S can be a bit like being a kid on
summer vacation. When you were young, we're guessing
that at some point, when you were out of school during
those long, hot months, you complained about being bored.
You probably got a fiery response from a busy parent who
had neither patience nor sympathy for your plight. It's
understandable why a kid could get bored during vacation.
During the school year, their lives are highly structured

and demanding. But for a kid on a rainy day in June, when all their friends are busy and there's nothing to watch on TV, having time affluence is almost a curse.

Most After-50s have fewer life demands than they did in Act I. If they had children, then by this point, their kids are getting more independent. Hopefully, they are beginning to vacate the house for college or careers. Aging parents might fill the obligation vacuum created by the exiting children, but even then, we're hoping that you have at least a bit more *Me Time*. And then there's another whole swath of After-50s who have retired. Their life demands have probably plummeted. They could be lost and antsy. So, we're comfortable with our comparison between the bored kid on summer vacation and the restless After-50. In the case of the bored kid, a parent will often say, *That's not my problem. Go outside and play!*

Boredom is often an unacknowledged problem for many After-50s. Our advice to avoid boredom is similar to the advice shared by the frustrated parent admonishing her child, albeit less harsh: You, too, definitely need to venture out and find a sense of engagement. The thing that After-50s simply must protect against is curiosity atrophy. This phase of life can be isolating. This phase of life can present unanticipated challenges that might make you want to wilt into obscurity. A joy-filled Act II life must be an engaged life. Engagement is the opposite of boredom.

THE HACK: DABBLE

Leon Battista Alberti is a wonderful figure who lived in fif-teenth-century Italy. Alberti is often seen as the Renaissance Man. He was an artist, athlete, and scholar. He was inter-ested in all things and a classic dabbler. You probably know people like this. They're fun to talk to and can enliven get-togethers. When you start pursuing engagement, you have the potential to morph into a modern Alberti. Being a Renaissance Person is the antithesis of being bored or boring. In an earlier Hack, we mentioned the objective of finding a reason to get up in the morning. When you're engaged in multiple activities in multiple realms, you wake up to a menu of options. You'll be fascinating to your cur-rent friends and attract new ones. What's more, you might start inspiring others who desperately need a role model.

Engagement certainly does not have to be physically strenuous. You can be engaged in your woodshop, in the kitchen, or on the Scrabble board as easily as you can on a hike through the woods. Do you have regular engaging activities that bring you joy? Do you have some activities that you really look forward to, and when you engage in them, time seems to evaporate? Are there skills you'd like to try? Even if your answers are no, we're here to help.

Let's try to be more bold, to venture out of our comfort zone, and to overcome obstacles. Just be willing to try new things. Once you start diving into potentially engaging new experiences and topics, you may find yourself in a place you couldn't have previously imagined. Your world could be fundamentally better and more interesting.

"My sister and her wife are my idea of Renaissance People. Julie and Lori worked as civil servants for many years before retiring. They deserve a quiet, peaceful Act II. They won't have it, though. Instead, they garden, paint, bake, remodel, fix, and build. They're in a wine club and travel often. They are dedicated caregivers and grandparents. They exercise and eat right. They never slow down; they engage and live healthy, joy-filled lives."

Pursuing engagement used to be so much harder. When we were young, obtaining information about any topic involved a lot of effort. One of the coolest truths about contemporary living is our unprecedented access to information. We can also collaborate globally with helpful guides. Be grateful for this. It makes diving into a topic much easier and more fruitful.

Our other massive attribute is time affluence, which we celebrate in many Hacks. After-50s simply have more time to explore, more time to investigate, and more time to dabble. Please try to always acknowledge this gift. The younger you would've loved this freedom.

So far, we've addressed you venturing out like a pioneer and finding engagement. We're also going to suggest another paradigm shift. Life presents obstacles and challenges. Some of these challenges, like the Bluetooth on your phone failing to connect to your sound system for a romantic dinner with your spouse, are merely annoying. But others, like losing a loved one, can be catastrophic. Perhaps, look at overcoming challenges as intellectual puzzles. This can represent a supreme form of dabbling. We've both experienced the devastation of losing loved ones, but upon reflection, we both grudgingly acknowledge that such tragedies inspired profound growth. We were different people a year after our losses—better people. When life presents such catastrophes, have faith that you'll eventually emerge from the grief stronger. This conviction will be of great comfort and utility. For less serious obstacles and challenges, like your bicycle tire going flat, instead of flying into boomer rage, welcome the challenge and commit yourself to fixing it. Keep asking yourself, *How can I fix this?* when:

- You get injured exercising
- Your kitchen table wobbles
- Your income is reduced when you retire
- Your automated recliner stops reclining
- Your cellphone bill is too high
- Your bedroom has too much artificial light
- You've become overweight

If you begin to think of such obstacles as opportunities, you may have fun solving your issues. You may develop confidence as someone who can fix things.

Also, as you dive into problem-solving mode, the journey

itself may take you down some fascinating paths that may spark new engagement opportunities. Fix the kitchen table and find a new fascination with woodworking. Find a more reasonable cellphone plan and trim the cost of your internet, your cable, and your electricity.

Another way to add engagement is to meet highly engaging people. In Hack 9, we'll tackle how to connect more, but for now, let's just focus on you. Your life, independent of anyone else, will be more engaging when you're curious about everything. Investigate ways to expand on the activities you enjoy. Speculate about how you could increase your exposure to new ideas and experiences. Concoct creative ways to monitor your progress toward goals.

WHAT YOU CAN DO TOMORROW

Not only is finding engaging activities enjoyable, but it also promotes brain health. The National Institute on Aging reinforced this idea in an article entitled "Cognitive Health and Older Adults." This resource suggested acquiring new hobbies and engaging in intellectually challenging activities—which could include problem-solving. Research points to such efforts as good for brain health. Let's begin tomorrow by setting the engagement table.

- **Read more; listen more.** We are both voracious readers, and we often read on the go. The advent of audiobooks, plus the ability to borrow a book virtually from the library, means that we both rarely walk or drive without being engaged by some melodious voice reading a book to us. The upshot is that we are exposed to so many great ideas at little or no cost. But this book selection should not be merely for entertainment—definitely go the nonfiction route. Choose a book that will inspire you to take action. Hopefully, this book has inspired you. If so, consume more nonfiction and grow. Reading has evolved our lives fundamentally. Search for books about any topic you have, or potentially have, a passion for. And if a book is not available on your desired topic, search for a podcast episode. We're confident you'll find a companion for your next walk.

- **Interview a practitioner.** No doubt, you still have a few role models in your life. Reach out to an After-50 who has an amazing life filled with engagement. It's not necessary for you to share their passions, whatever they are; what's important is that you talk to them and ask them questions. Invite them for coffee and pick their brain. They may be honored that someone like you is impressed with them. Ask them what they do most days, how they discovered their passions, what they would like to do next, and how pursuing their passions has impacted their lives. And finally, if they agree to have coffee with you, they probably know you pretty well. Ask them if they have any advice on how you could be more engaged in life.

- **Fix something.** This isn't sexy, but it's quite powerful. If you're like us, there's a to-do list on your refrigerator. These are typically difficult, complicated, and frustrating tasks that you can never seem to bring yourself to do. Tomorrow, choose one that you dread and do it. Come at this task with a clear mind and a clear heart. You're an intelligent person, you've tackled many challenges in your life, and there's no reason why fixing a loose faucet or changing a bicycle tire should intimidate you. You have the internet and the local hardware store for support.

Mastering this challenge may turn out to be more enjoyable than you think, particularly because you're listening to a great book on your phone as you tinker away.

- **Set a goal.** Think about an aspect of your life that you'd like to change. Perhaps you'd like to lose weight or improve your cardio health. Maybe you'd like to meet new people. It could be that the Midwest winters have worn you out and you want to move down South each year during a couple of the coldest months, or the overwhelming heat in Texas has you heading north for a reprieve. Perhaps you have less money if you're retired, and you need to adjust by creating a new budget. Make this goal so important that if you achieve it, you will vastly improve your life. Achieving this goal may take time, but all we want you to do tomorrow is figure out what you'd like to change or master. Satisfying this goal could generate much confidence in the long term, but all we're concerned about tomorrow is your focus on a goal.

BUILDING MOMENTUM

Let's find some ways you can be more engaged during this potentially awesome phase of life. This engagement can be physical, intellectual, creative, or emotional. What engages you can be as unique as your fingerprints, or it could have wide appeal. Pursuing it can lead to new and exciting relationships. When you meet new people who are engaged in some of the same activities as you, it's certainly easy to find topics to talk about.

Step 1: Try a new activity for three weeks.

There's a lingering belief that if you engage in any desirable activity, such as exercise, for twenty-one days straight, it'll be habit-forming. If you search for this idea online, you'll be greeted with plenty of results with titles such as *Busting the 21-Day Habit Myth*. That's too bad because twenty-one days doesn't seem like much of a commitment. Unfortunately, research points to a longer habit-forming transition—much longer. But we still think the twenty-one-day window has value, not in terms of behavior modification, but in terms of evaluating your engagement to whatever you'd like to try. Three weeks is a great testing ground. If you decide to make three healthy meals a week for the next three weeks, we predict that after this time period, you'll have a good feel for whether you want to continue. So, for the next twenty-one days, give something you've been wanting to try, a try. Then, evaluate the experience. If it didn't live up to your expectations, bag it. But if you like it and decide to continue, you may be laying the groundwork for a positive new habit.

Step 2: Become a student again.

One of the most empowering steps you can take is to commit to learning again. Often, when a college freshman meets with their advisor for the first time to create a class schedule, the advisor will paint a picture of the university as an oyster, and the student's mission will be to investigate all the possibilities in search of the elusive pearl. We love this analogy and the disposition of youthful wonder and possibility that it invokes. If you're like us, some incredible learning opportunities were missed thanks to the arrogance of youth. Well, now you have the time to learn whatever you like, and your choice of venues is diverse. Many institutions of higher learning welcome older students and allow them to audit courses at little or no cost. This may not be enough for you. You may be so motivated that you pay the tuition in pursuit of a degree. Bravo! Or you may decide that becoming a formal student is not necessary. You can take classes at Home Depot, your local library, your church, or other local organizations. Merely decide what you'd like to learn and then find a teacher or a program. And don't forget YouTube, which has morphed into the world's teacher on how to do pretty much anything.

> "In my dabbling quests, I've been utilizing free artificial intelligence platforms that are now available. These highly intuitive tools will guide you in achieving goals and fixing problems. I've learned how to eliminate clover from my yard, rehab from an athletic injury, and design great lesson plans. We live in a remarkable age. Remember that the next time one of your contemporaries is complaining about modern life."

Step 3: Teach someone else your new skill.

As we prompted in the Introduction, *You teach best what you most need to learn.* So if, for example, you want to become more proficient at candle-making or landscaping, guilt one of your friends into indulging you by becoming your student. Morph them into candle-making or landscaping disciples. Don't fret over your ulterior motive. Your buddy may catch candle-making or landscaping fever. You could make their lives more engaging in the process. And even if they don't join your engagement tribe, you'll learn a lot about your passion by attempting to teach it to them.

Step 4: Quantify your growth.

You may balk at this suggestion. Attaching data to an activity that's supposed to be fun and engaging does not seem like it would contribute to enjoyment. But please hear us out. James Clear, the author of *Atomic Habits*, claims that *what we measure, we improve.* This assertion is certainly worth a try. If you're regularly engaged in an activity, you probably have a goal to improve in that area. How you keep track of progress is up to you, but our intuition tells us that doing so would support growth. You could even make a game of it. You could formulate predictions about how many books you'll read this month or how many hours of quality sleep you'll average. When you create such targets, it can lend clarity to your efforts.

Jim knows a retired couple obsessed with budgeting. They've managed their money well their whole lives, but their incomes have declined in retirement. They have plenty of money and don't need to do this, but they created a game. They each get a monthly allowance. They plan their discretionary purchases, and they also take full advantage of discounts and rebates. They take wonderful vacations and still spend for enjoyment, but they refuse to waste their resources. Whoever has the most allowance money at the end of the month treats the vanquished with a small gift. It's fun to have a goal to strive toward. Make certain you reward yourself once you achieve it.

Step 5: Master a new skill.

We absolutely love this suggestion. Not only could you build confidence by mastering a new skill, but you could also save a lot of money. What do you currently pay people to do? It could be cleaning your home, treating your lawn, doing your taxes, maintaining your car, or painting your walls. A few of these services may be beyond you, but consider learning how to do one thing that you currently pay someone to provide, and then do it yourself. This could give you a wonderful sense of achievement, and when you're proficient in this task, you may do it even better than the people you used to pay.

REMOVING OBSTACLES

Pursuing engagement takes courage. You may have to step out of your comfort zone and look foolish as you attempt to grapple with new ideas, new skills, and new experiences. But your hesitancy might entail more than a generic reluctance to venture into the unknown. Consider these roadblocks and their workarounds.

I can't think of any activities that interest me. This is a common emotion we've both experienced. There are stretches of life when you just don't feel adventurous. It's okay to go through such phases. In the analogy at the beginning of this Hack, with the bored kid during summer vacation, the frustrated parent orders the youngster to go outside and play. That's still good advice. Sometimes you have to get off the spot and get out of your comfort zone and give something a try. Intuitively, you know this is true. You've probably given this advice to others. If you're this far through this Hack, we hope you've been convinced that pursuing engagement could enrich your life. As uncomfortable as it may be to try or to explore unfamiliar areas, you'll grow just from the experience of trying. And, in the process, you may find a new passion.

I don't like to do things I'm not good at. We get it on this front too. When you try new activities, like going back to school after decades, you are probably going to initially feel like a fish out of water. When you attempt to throw your first pot in an adult art class, it may look like a lopsided vessel that a kindergartner would produce. But so what. No one, and we truly mean no one, expects you to be proficient at any novel activity. These are totally self-imposed expectations. Please relax and be present as you experience life. These are low-stakes adventures with potentially big payoffs. It's okay not to be a star at something. Not having lofty expectations is a lot less stressful. We've both had to work hard at overcoming this emotion.

All of this sounds expensive. This is a legitimate concern. When you dive down a new rabbit hole, it can be expensive. We have two reactions to this reservation. Our first is that spending money on experiences is a magnificent investment. The shirt we purchased ten years ago? We donated it because we no longer wear it. The hiking vacation we took with our spouses ten years ago? We still talk about the trip, and it serves as an inspiration to take another such adventure. If you have the discretionary resources, then pursuing engagement is an excellent way to allocate some of them. If you don't have a massive retirement nest egg, and believe us when we say we're both pretty frugal, then investigate ways to pursue engagement that are free or low cost, such as auditing a class at a university, attending inexpensive classes in your community, reading, or watching YouTube tutorials.

I want to relax. This sounds like work. Okay, if you feel this way, we don't have as much sympathy for you. When you're engaged in a wonderful new activity, it doesn't seem like work. Many artists and athletes refer to being in the "flow." This is a state when one is immersed in a game or in the creative process. When you're in the flow, outside stimuli like time awareness and background noise evaporate. If you get into a flow with a new activity, you may look up and be amazed that it's almost time to eat dinner. This is a magical place to be. We're all for relaxing, but earn that relaxation by experiencing a stimulating day where you try something new.

THE HACK IN ACTION

Pursuing engagement does not need to be expensive or time-consuming. It can be a lot of fun—remember the directive to go outside and play? Engagement can come from the most unexpected places, and if you're open enough to experiment, you'll find it.

Jim's story …

My wife and I recently visited an educational science museum. You know, the type of place where you put your hand on an electrified ball and your hair stands on end. As we meandered through the exhibits, we found an interesting contraption that measured your balance. You were challenged to stand on these steel foot pedals and see how long you could keep either pedal from clanking against the ground. The longer you could hover without clanking, the better your balance. As you can probably surmise, my wife and I did not do too great on this assessment. This was sobering because balance is a major concern for After-50s. When you become unstable, you're susceptible to falls. I knew as I walked out of the museum that I would dive down an improving-balance rabbit hole.

I purchased a wobble board on Amazon for less than twenty bucks. This board is a large wooden circle. Below it is a small circular plastic base. The idea is to stand on the board and levitate, not allowing the edges of the board to touch the floor. At first, I was a terrible wobble boarder, but I improved rapidly. I worked on it for a few minutes each morning after my workout. After I developed some balance, confidence, and competence, I gamified my efforts. I started to time how long I could levitate. Each day, I tried to outlast the previous day's record. Most days, I improved. I became so full of myself that I started to experiment with balancing on one leg. I got better at that too.

My wobble board experience has been great fun. It takes about five minutes each day, and I've been able to measure my marked improvement. It involved very little expense. Improving my balance has boosted my confidence.

AFTER 50s _Life_

We encourage dabbling because we love the idea of you rediscovering, or perhaps developing for the first time, a curiosity about the world. Acquiring such a desire may involve an attitude adjustment. Dabbling may involve trial and error, but we believe such a disposition will inspire you to overcome obstacles, try new ideas, and meet new people. Sinking into prolonged boredom and complacency is a real threat to After-50s. Let's make certain this doesn't happen to you.

Hack 9

CONNECT

You're not done making friends

*The most terrible poverty is loneliness
and the feeling of being unloved.*
— MOTHER TERESA, FOUNDER OF
MISSIONARIES OF CHARITY

THE PROBLEM: YOU'RE FEELING ISOLATED

LIFE AFTER FIFTY can be lonely. This is not only sad, but it can also be dangerous. The Centers for Disease Control and Prevention, in an online article titled "Loneliness and Social Isolation Linked to Serious Health Conditions," equated social isolation's health impact to standard villains of longevity such as smoking and obesity. This is a sobering claim. It's time to recognize that isolation, aside from being tragic, is also a threat to health.

Think of all the events that can happen after age fifty that accelerate this isolation:

- Your kids leave home.

- You retire and then miss your coworkers.

- You lose physical mobility, so you aren't as active.

- A relationship dissolves.

- A dear friend moves to be close to their kids.

- Your aged parent dies.

- A beloved sibling dies.

- Your friends start to die.

- Your dog dies.

- Your spouse dies.

- Your familiar neighborhood doesn't seem familiar anymore because your friends are downsizing and moving away.

This list was so easy to make and not meant to be exhaustive. It could go on and on. One of the cruelest aspects to aging is that, as you get older, these isolating factors grow exponentially. When you reminisce about aging and deceased friends and family, you start to wonder, *Will I be the last one standing?* In this life stage, attending and planning memorial services become a painful reality.

One factor that can exacerbate feelings of isolation and loneliness, not to mention envy, is social media. We know many contemporaries who doom-scroll on Facebook almost nightly. They peruse self-promotional posts from acquaintances who seem to have it all. They're off on magnificent vacations, their beautiful families arrange themselves perfectly for group photos at celebrations and holidays, and their carefully selected photos and profile pics make them look twenty years younger.

Please understand that there's probably lots of drama hidden behind these highly scripted and curated billboards of domestic bliss. They likely aren't nearly as content, and their families nearly as congenial, as they look. Your nightly Facebook journeys could, unfortunately, act as painful reminders of everything you don't have and everything you aren't. Such emotions can contribute to feelings of isolation. But we don't want to come off as hypocrites in terms of social media. We've posted self-promotionally. It's fun to share photos you're proud of and have friends celebrate your achievement. Social media also has wonderful aspects and can reunite lost friends and foster new relationships, but we've come to recognize the negative side of these powerful tools. These platforms should serve us, not make us feel bad. We can help you use social media in ways that serve you.

"Social media does have the power to facilitate new relationships and nurture old ones. A great tactic is to utilize direct messaging. My favorite DM strategies are to send a congratulation when a friend shares an accomplishment (even if I'm a little envious) and a condolence when a friend faces a hardship or loss. My experience has been that such messages make the recipients feel good and lead to more interactions between them and me. That's a great use of social media."

Coming to grips with the bitter realities of this life stage and dealing with feelings of envy that everyone else is thriving because of what they post on social media is hard enough. What's doubly challenging is to figure out how to break out of your After-50s isolation and rejoin the world. If you're retired, you've lost the social interaction opportunity that came by default at work each day. If you're not retired, you know what to expect in your not-too-distant future. Are you cognizant that the extensive social network you interact with daily will dwindle to a trickle? What preparations are you making for this loss? The previous sentence articulates what we'll attempt to do in this Hack.

Meeting and socializing with people probably happened organically for most of your life. You met people at work. You met people at church. You met people through your kid's activities. You became friends with your neighbors who were at a similar life stage. Now that you're after fifty, it's important for you to be intentional about connecting. The same skill sets you utilized when you were younger to find the right job or the right spouse can now be resurrected and then adapted to the goal of finding new friends. The great news is that, compared to interviewing for a job or proposing to a potential spouse, finding new friends after fifty is a low-stakes aspiration. If you attempt to connect with a new friend and the interaction fizzles, you're out virtually nothing and you can learn a lot about how to improve your search filter. And, you're not attempting to find just one dream job or just one soulmate. There's a lot less pressure when you're just trying to interact with more people and find new friends.

THE HACK: CONNECT

It's helpful to think about connection as capital. When economists talk about capital, they're referring to assets. Acquiring new friends *is* acquiring new assets. New friends are valuable. They can make you happier and healthier. They can be there for you in a crisis. You can be as beneficial to them as they are to you. We have plenty of friends who are contemporaries and consider us as assets. So we're going to stick with our analogy.

As we mentioned in The Problem section of this Hack, our desire is to spark intentionality about connecting. That's not to say that new friendships cannot blossom organically; we just don't want you to sit idly by, waiting for someone else to make the first move. That probably didn't work decades ago at your high school dances unless, of course, you were smoking hot, and it probably won't work at this stage of life. We aim to give you some ideas, but we're more concerned with helping you find the motivation and the confidence to step out of your comfort zone and make the first move. We won't just yell, *Get over your fears and get out there!* Instead, we want to inspire you to get out there in your own time and in your own way.

To bond with others, you need to be approachable. Have you ever evaluated your approachability? Do you broadcast a welcoming vibe? Would you feel comfortable meeting you? These are important questions, and adjustments in this realm could be instrumental in achieving a broader social network.

As with all the Hacks in this book, we encourage you to create your own goals and your own roadmap to expand your connections—and we'll offer many suggestions along the way. This is ultimately your journey, but sometimes you need a nudge in the right direction. This Hack works hand-in-hand with Hack 8. Often, the pursuit of engagement leads to opportunities to expand your social interactions with like-minded people. As with engagement, networking is an invaluable tool.

And finally, even though the focus of this Hack is to grow your social network, you probably have more relationships than you think. Those bonds with friends and family need to be nurtured and maintained. Please don't take these important folks for granted.

WHAT YOU CAN DO TOMORROW

The loneliness that often accompanies life after fifty can be compared to a relationship breakup. The relationship in our analogy represents all the social interactions you had when you were younger. The breakup represents diminished opportunities to meet and greet as you sail past fifty. Most of us have experienced painful breakups. Trusted friends and family members nudged us back out into the dating pool. We needed those nudges. As awkward as it may seem to you, we're going to encourage you to put yourself back out there into the social interaction pool, too, and start forging new relationships.

- **Interact.** Typically, when you pursue engagement, you realize the potential for new social interaction. And, the folks you meet when engaged in an activity will probably be interested in the same things as you. You'll automatically have important commonalities. This is an essential ingredient for any budding friendship. Go back over your list of ideas of activities you'd like to try in pursuit of engagement. Then, consider how each could place you in a situation where you might meet new people. Consider how you'll respond if such a situation presents itself.

- **Chat with a stranger.** You may be reluctant to talk to people you don't know. The idea of it might make you uncomfortable. You might be worried that it's unsafe or you'll send the wrong message. If this suggestion is a bridge too far for you—we understand. But we are not talking about deep or intimate conversations. All we want you to do is get accustomed to smiling and saying *Hi* to people you don't know. You don't even have to break stride. If you make eye contact with someone at the grocery, just smile and greet them, and then you can keep on trucking. Or, if you walk into a building in front of someone, hold the door for them, whether they are male or female, and invite them out of the elements. If you're in line and ready to purchase an item, and you get a pleasant vibe from a line mate, ask them about an item they are purchasing. You may learn about a cool product. These interactions will help you reactivate social muscles that may have atrophied. These are short, low-stakes social excursions. What we love about doing this is that whether or not we get much back in return, chatting with strangers puts us in a better mood.

"I didn't used to be a very social person. I'd even avoid neighbors. After reading How to Talk to Anyone *by Leil Lowndes, I decided to take some chances and strike up conversations with people I'd bump into on walks. Lowndes's advice is to look for common points of interest and start there. I saw a neighbor gardening, and I stopped and joked that I had some gardening work she could do since hers was so beautiful and mine was hideous. This led to a lovely five-minute conversation and a neighbor I now speak to regularly."*

- **Interview a trusted friend.** Invite a dear friend to meet over coffee. Explain to them that you're going to pick their brain on a project that you're passionate about. After you've sat down, slurped some java, and caught up, tell them about your objective to have more social interaction, and ask if they can help you in this quest by answering some questions. Ask them about the origins of your relationship. Here are some suggestions:

▸ What was your first impression of me?

▸ What did we talk about early in our friendship?

▸ How did we meet?

▸ When did you first start to consider me a friend?

▸ How does my friendship serve you?

▸ How could I become a better friend to you?

▸ How could I become more approachable?

▸ Do you have any ideas on how I could meet people?

▸ Would you be willing to join me when I go on a new experience?

We love these questions. If you muster the courage to ask them, you may learn a lot about yourself in the process. Regardless, you and your friend will probably have a wonderful time reminiscing, and you'll strengthen the bond between you two.

- **Evaluate your employment status.**
  You need to start this process in earnest tomorrow. If you're working, start evaluating

how long you want to work. Get serious about this question. The more specific you can get about when to retire, the more potential you'll have to exert some control over when and how it happens. Working or not working is a major factor regarding social interaction. Consider how you'll replace interactions with others when you retire. If you are retired, evaluate how you feel about not working when it comes to social interaction. If you have plenty of social interaction and are retired, congratulations! But many aren't so fortunate. Going back to work, working part time, or volunteering are options. If you're feeling isolated, spend time tomorrow considering these three options from the perspective of how they would impact social interaction.

- **Evaluate your living status.** While you're evaluating your working life, go ahead and evaluate your living situation as well. This one has the potential to be emotional, particularly if you've lived somewhere for a long time. Financial factors may trump any such evaluation, but tomorrow, just consider the following: *Is my living situation conducive*

> *to social interaction?* This is a challenging and important question. We both struggle on this front. We both live in large houses where we raised families. We have a deep sense of comfort and belonging in our homes. We invested equity and sweat equity in these houses. But do they still fit our purposes? Are our homes isolating us? Should we downsize? Should we move to a 55-plus community? Should we move to a new state? Questions about your working life or your living situation will probably not be answered right away, but you can start evaluating both in earnest tomorrow.

BUILDING MOMENTUM

We confess that we've been approaching this idea of expanding connections in a self-serving fashion—we're advancing ideas to help you thrive after age fifty. But maybe we should share a more altruistic approach. A magnificent way to consider this perspective is to study the Grandmother Effect. Check out "Living Near Your Grandmother Has Evolutionary Benefits" on the NPR health and development blog *Goats and Soda*. This well-researched theory posits that children and mothers thrive when grandmas are close by. This proximity also gives the grandma a healthy dose of social interaction and a feeling of being needed. This is a classic win-win proposition. The lesson for all After-50s is that you can help others profoundly, and then you simultaneously benefit from the effort. Keep that in mind as you aim to expand your connections.

Step 1: Facilitate.

The wise saying, *If you want something done right—do it yourself,* certainly applies here. Your family has needs. Your friends have needs. Your community has needs. This world has needs. Perhaps, you can help. Here are a few ideas for your inner facilitator:

- Make a recurring lunch date with colleagues you used to work with. They probably miss you and each other.

- Start a book club with some folks you haven't seen in a while. We have a friend who did this, and he gets intellectual stimulation and camaraderie.

- Launch a watch party. This could be for sporting events, favorite shows, or a new movie.

These examples are good and can help people you know feel more connected. Some problems are more profound. You might turn into a lifesaver if you facilitate the following:

- Volunteer at your school with at-risk kids.

- Help refugees acquire citizenship.

- Serve as a mentor to a parolee.

- Volunteer at a community health clinic in a house of worship.

- Encourage a friend to attend grief counseling, drive them to sessions, and participate in the meeting. (Jim knows a woman who did this. She's also a widow, and the positive impact on her was significant.)

Keep asking yourself, *What needs to be done? How can I help?*

Step 2: Fix a regret.

If you're over the age of fifty, you certainly have regrets. You may suffer from haunting memories. You wish that you could briefly turn back the hands of time and make different choices. You've probably hurt other people. If you can conjure up no examples of when you made miserable choices, then you are a far better person than either of us.

You have a number of options to cope with these emotions:

- Apologize and make amends. This is a powerful option but not always possible. The person you wronged may be deceased or unavailable.

They may react badly to your overture. These are potentially dangerous waters, and only you can decide if you should choose to embark on this voyage. But we can say that when we have apologized for past actions, in the majority of cases, it has been well received. In some cases, it led to the restoration of a relationship. Even when it doesn't go as well as you hoped, you'll probably eject some negative emotions surrounding your regret.

- Vow to treat people better. Even if you choose not to apologize for past sins, you could pledge to avoid treating people in the way that caused your regret. Every person you interact with will benefit from this effort.

The redemptive prescriptions in this step are powerful. They can heal damaged relationships, facilitate new ones, and make the world a better place.

Step 3: Save a pet.

We absolutely hated researching the data for this step. We were not surprised by what we found, and it's tragic. Three-quarters of a million unwanted dogs and cats are euthanized in the United States each year. The suffering and the lost potential for love and two-way companionship breaks our hearts. We have no illusions about what a major undertaking it is to adopt a pet. We've rescued dogs. We've cleaned up messes. We've had things torn up.

We've juggled schedules and made logistic arrangements to care for animals while we went on vacation. But maybe, adopting a pet could be one of the most therapeutic actions you can take. Dogs and cats are spectacular creatures. It's as if they've evolved to love us. If you treat your rescued animals well, and many have trauma that you'll have to navigate, they will grow to adore you. It's great to be loved. American Humane points to research that shows specific health benefits to seniors who own pets, and these benefits include lower blood pressure and more physical activity, which will help heart health. This may be the last responsibility you want at this stage of life. You survived child-rearing, and now you have the freedom that an empty nest brings. But if you're lonely, please consider rescuing a pet. This wonderful animal will love you unconditionally.

Step 4: Go virtual.

If you're searching for romance, online dating services work for many. According to Pew Research, 30 percent of Americans have utilized such a platform, and 12 percent have married or been in a committed relationship with someone they've met online. Those numbers were higher than we thought, but our surprise is understandable. We both are old enough and have been married long enough to find the whole idea of meeting a romantic partner this way novel. But we are certainly not opposed to this phenomenon. We love the transparency of the effort. Every participant knows exactly why every other participant is on the site. What's true for those seeking romance can also be true for After-50s seeking more social interaction. A meetup group is a collection of like-minded individuals who typically find each other virtually, then meet in person or virtually and indulge in their shared passions. Online matching platforms will pair you based on your interests with like-minded people. You can also find entire platforms dedicated specifically to matching up older folks—not just for romance but also for companionship. This option is worth exploring.

Step 5: Treat yourself.

We totally stole this idea from the magnificent workplace sitcom *Parks and Recreation*. In season 4, episode 4, two of the main characters go on an epic indulgence spree. They purchase luxury items and expensive treatments. While the show makes fun of how self-centered they're behaving, there is a subtle nod to the idea that indulging is a well-earned reward. Don't hesitate to do the same. You don't have to wait for someone to join you at the natural history museum, botanical garden, statehouse tour, or ballgame. Going solo is better than sitting at home. You might find that you enjoy these activities alone. You also might meet someone cool who's there on their own as well.

REMOVING OBSTACLES

In this Hack, we ask you to take some pretty bold steps— steps that may make you uncomfortable. We wouldn't propose such unless we believed the potential payoff was worth it. But you may still feel some reservations, including the ones we list here.

I'm shy. This can be a significant obstacle. If you took the Myers-Briggs Personality Test, you might have scored a solid "I" for introvert. Meeting people, talking to strangers, and initiating conversations are not your strengths. But please look at the problem of loneliness objectively. If you find yourself in a situation that is not acceptable, you have to make changes. Not making changes and hoping interesting people will find you by extending themselves will likely not happen. We put forth ideas in this Hack, but they're just suggestions. We're more interested in you extending yourself and coming up with your own pre-scriptions. Putting yourself out there may be uncomfort-able, but the potential payoff is worth it.

This seems forced. Yes, extending yourself to meet others is a bit forced. But your life circumstances change after fifty. We are not suggesting that you won't meet anyone organi-cally at this life stage. What we are suggesting is that for most, the opportunities to meet people organically are not nearly as robust, so we need to be proactive about it.

I think I'll get discouraged. Discouragement can impede growth. You may have read some of our ideas for expanding your connections and come away unimpressed. Or, you may give one of our ideas, or one that you con-coct, a try, and it falls flat. You may start to feel desperate and worry that you are doomed to a solitary existence in this last portion of life. But we challenge you to resist this interpretation. Success typically involves trial and error. Billions of people live in the world, and meeting like-minded people is a numbers game. If you extend yourself to a handful of new potential friends and it's an unsuccessful effort, don't give up, thinking that it's impossible. That would not be thinking objectively. Expanding your social network may take time. Please be patient.

My current friends will get jealous. If you feel this way, the great news is that at least you have friends who will feel such emotions. Our idea is for you to be transparent with them about your goals and then invite them along on this adventure. If they're jealous, they are probably experiencing some loneliness too.

THE HACK IN ACTION

Life can change abruptly after fifty. These changes can be welcomed or unwelcomed. It's important to attempt to be as flexible as possible and to keep experimenting.

Jim's story ...

I was fifty-eight, and I had taught high school social studies for decades. I was past my retirement age, but I was reluctant to take this bold step. I was still vibrant and enjoyed the job. I loved my students and my place in the community. When I went to the grocery store, I greeted and interacted with numerous folks—students and former students and parents. I loved this part of my life.

And then suddenly, in March of that year, everything changed. My district offered a buyout to veteran teachers. The cash settlement was significant, and retirement was an event I was anticipating by age sixty. But I was hesitant. How in the world could I replace all the wonderful interactions I got at school each day? My schedule had been packed with social interaction. I had just shy of 150 students in my classes, which didn't include study hall or lunch duty. What would replace this?

On a lark, I contacted the Education Department chair at a local university. I was friends with this woman, and she encouraged me to adjunct there, working with future educators. I took her up on her suggestion and retired from my high school teaching job. Teaching college has been a wonderful transition. I don't interact with nearly the same number of students—but I enjoy them as much as I did my high school students. I only teach two days a week. But I have much more freedom. The college calendar is more forgiving, and I'm free most days of the week. It was a good decision.

But when I go to the local grocery now, I'm no longer a celebrity. In retirement, I've had to work to expand my connections. I'm not satisfied, and I have more work to do. There are times when I feel lonely and discouraged. I also know that I won't be an adjunct forever, and that will represent another transition. My goal is to remain open and keep experimenting by putting myself out there.

AFTER 50s *Life*

We take so much for granted when we are younger. Most youngsters can move pain-free. They're strong, mobile, and fast. Many younger folks have reservations about aging and losing this physical vitality. Still, we hear many thirty- and forty-somethings wax eloquently about all they will do with the freedom of their After-50s lives when their daily obligations have diminished. This is a classic tradeoff. What we rarely hear is their anticipation about the obstacle that loneliness can erect for After-50s. This can be a profound problem. Hopefully, this Hack gave you ideas about how to master this obstacle.

THRIVE

Ramp up your zest for life

My mission in life is not merely to survive, but to thrive; and to do so with some passion, some compassion, some humor, and some style.
— MAYA ANGELOU, MEMOIRIST, POET, AND ACTIVIST

THE PROBLEM: AFTER-50S CAN LOSE THEIR ZEST FOR LIFE

ABOUT 280 MILLION people in the world suffer from depression, according to the WHO (the World Health Organization, not the rock band). More than sixteen million of them are After-50s. They have feelings of low self-worth, loss of pleasure, and thoughts of dying. It's not at all unusual for After-50s, especially those aged seventy or older, to feel like the end is near. And facing a malady like diabetes or cancer can make depression and mood swings exponentially worse. Additionally, you may be transitioning from one career to another, retiring, fighting chronic pain, going through a divorce, or grieving the loss of a friend or family member. These physical and emotional problems can suck the zest out of life, making it easy to give up.

You may wonder, *What's left for me?*

THE HACK: THRIVE

Most of this book is about thriving, using what we call a Momentum Mindset. We've tried to be as transparent as possible, reminding you that we're not doctors or nutritionists; we are practitioners. While we certainly have bad days, replete with anger, frustration, and sadness, we focus on our Momentum Mindsets and employ some combination of the strategies in prior Hacks. The more strategies you use individually or stacked, the more you'll flourish in your After-50s life. Remember, embedded in thriving in life's Act II is the concept of momentum. Focus on forward motion in all areas we've discussed, and you will thrive.

WHAT YOU CAN DO TOMORROW

One definition of thriving includes the phrase "growing vigorously." To grow, you need the kind of momentum we've discussed throughout this book. Let's revisit some earlier strategies and build the momentum we need to overcome sadness, anxiety, fatigue, and anything else ruining your zest for life.

- **Get moving.** In Hack 4, we emphasize the value of movement—of almost any kind. We quote the WHO (still not the rock band), which emphasizes the deleterious effect of a sedentary life including, but not limited to, physical and emotional trauma. The simplest path to thriving in life's Act II is to get moving, especially when you feel sad. Just get up on your feet. Reach for the sky, get on your toes, and take a few steps. This act will be like priming your energy pump. A few steps will help lubricate everything. Build off this. Go outside in the sunshine and take a walk in your neighborhood, or follow a virtual yoga teacher through a workout, or maybe even do some body-weight resistance exercises. You'll be glad you got moving.

- **Face grief head-on.** Nothing kills one's zest for living faster than grief. While you can do this tomorrow (or even today), we wouldn't dare suggest that overcoming grief is easy. Dealing with a debilitating illness, transitioning from a long career, losing someone dear to you, or the universal grief that comes with aging can bring paralyzing sadness. We have faced most kinds of grief throughout our lives, including having family members with mental illness, battling pain and disease, and burying loved ones. While psychologists and grief experts offer an array of coping strategies, varying based on from where the grief stems, we have found that facing grief head-on is the best way to cope in the short and, eventually, long term. Reflect on what's causing the pain. Put steps in place to fight illness, learn how to help your troubled family members, and celebrate lost loved ones. When grief strikes for any reason, revisit Hack 6, Nurture. The strategies there have worked well for us, and they can work for you too.

- **Resist negativity.** Politics and a pandemic, among other issues, have divided people and spread toxicity around the world. We see hate everywhere, especially on social media. We won't tell you to never surf Facebook, Instagram, or other popular social networks; we dabble in these spaces periodically. To thrive, though, it's crucial that you avoid negativity, as it is damaging to your mental and physical well-being. If you're a political person, feel free to campaign. We hope you vote. Please steer clear, though, of hot-button discussions online. As author Dale Carnegie wrote, you can never win an argument. We believe truer words have never been spoken. You don't have to agree with everyone, and you can share your opinions. Avoid heated debates and scroll past toxic memes, and you'll feed your soul and, likely, add years of joy to your life.

"I don't let politics influence my day. I'm informed, I vote, and I even contribute to candidates, but I'll be darned if I'm going to let politics influence my mood or how I interact with loved ones. I have an app on my phone that provides articles from both sides of the spectrum. I peruse this app twice a day, and that's it. Politics does not pollute my life."

- **Refuel your body.** In Hack 3, we provided strategies for improving your diet without completely eliminating the foods you love.

When you're feeling down and need a momentum burst, grab a healthy snack rather than a bag of potato chips or a candy bar. Apples, bananas, berries, and mixed nuts are your best friends at this moment. Eat a healthy snack when you need to thrive, and you'll get an immediate boost of energy, along with a smile on your face.

- **Recharge your brain.** Few things go better with your effort to thrive than restorative sleep, covered in depth in Hack 7. One of the best ways to stamp out sadness is to recharge your body and brain as quickly as possible. There's no faster way to do this than with restorative sleep. Need a little zest in your week? Plan an impactful night of sleep, and follow all steps in Hack 7 to make it happen.

- **Engage.** (Hat tip to Captain Jean-Luc Picard from Star Trek, who vaulted his ship to warp with this simple, powerful word.) Hack 8 is all about engaging with friends, colleagues, community, work, and even content. When you need to thrive, engaging is a foolproof way to bring back the zest.

- **Give.** With thriving comes good feelings about yourself. Few efforts can make you feel better than giving to others. This doesn't mean donating to your favorite charity, although that's certainly worthwhile. You can give time to someone in need by volunteering or just showing up. You can give support to a friend, colleague, or loved one; let them know you're there—a shoulder to lean on. You can give someone a hug. You can give a smile to that passerby on the street. These small endeavors matter, and they'll absolutely help you thrive.

- **Touch.** As simple as this strategy may seem, it's arguably the most impactful thing you can do in your quest for health, longevity, and joy. Human touch is a basic need. Many studies tout the power of holding hands and giving or receiving a six-second hug. The impact of sex on mental and physical fitness has been studied for decades, and research indicates that many people enjoy healthy sex lives well into their eighties. If you're eager to thrive in your After-50s life, what better way than to hug your spouse or significant other and regularly take that hug a good bit further.

BUILDING MOMENTUM

Thriving and building momentum are almost synonymous. Both imply growth and motion. "Thrive" means to flourish or prosper. So, how do you build momentum toward thriving? In full transparency, you've learned this already in the prior nine Hacks. We've referenced some of the strategies in the What You Can Do Tomorrow section, and we elaborate here.

Step 1: Revisit your morning routine.

Thriving starts in the morning the moment you get out of bed (hopefully, after a wonderfully restorative night of sleep). We've mentioned the power of mornings in numerous Hacks. To thrive, start every morning with movement (simple stretches or yoga poses will do just fine). Get outside and soak up some sun (if there is any to be had) as soon as possible (a brisk walk in the sunshine before your morning coffee or tea is perfect). Add deep, mindful breathing (this can also be part of that fabulous walk). If you're battling anxiety, fatigue, or grief, this simple morning routine will help you shake out the cobwebs and rev up momentum for the rest of your day.

Step 2: Focus on purpose.

Whether you're fifty, seventy, or ninety, you have a purpose. It may not be to show up for work, or to raise your kids, or to run a marathon. It may be a purpose that seems insignificant to other people. Big or small, sophisticated or simple, your purpose fuels your Momentum Mindset and is crucial for you to thrive throughout your life's Act II. Your purpose is what gets you out of bed each day. It's your *Why*. If you're still working, your purpose may be your career or community work. If you're retired and traveling the world, this gives you purpose—embrace the journey as if it's the last thing you'll ever do. If you've moved to an independent living facility, your purpose might be to make new friends and contribute to this community, helping people there to thrive. If you're growing your garden, it's up to you to make the plants, flowers, and vegetables thrive, and this is an important purpose; who else will nurture this living flora but you? If you've moved to the beach or the mountains, you may strive to commune with nature as you never have. You may be searching for spirituality. This striving and searching gives you purpose. Contemplate your purpose and focus on it every day.

Step 3: Plan get-togethers.

We've talked about community throughout this book. You have one, several, or many communities, and they play a role in your health and well-being. Whether it's your family, friends, church group, golf league, or book club, plan regular get-togethers with a community. One of the most underrated contributors to health and longevity is spending time with friends and loved ones. Don't wait for an invite. After-50s with a Momentum Mindset are action-oriented; reach out to your community today and plan regular get-togethers. It can be a shared meal, a cup of coffee, or a short walk. No matter how you dedicate the time or how much time it is, spending it with people will help you thrive.

> "My late father-in-law understood the value of engaging with people. He and a small group of friends started a weekly poker night nearly a half-century ago. They rarely missed a Friday night. I was fortunate to join them once. Apart from losing my money to these veteran card sharps, what I remember most was the feeling of camaraderie among them. They helped me understand the power of engagement."

Step 4: Accentuate the positive.

When you spend time with a community, do not underestimate the power of the attitudes of each community member. According to Dan Buettner, author of *Blue Zones: 9 Lessons for Living Longer From the People Who've Lived the Longest*, you're more likely to thrive when you build relationships with positive people. In his many years of studying centenarians, Buettner learned that people in Okinawa, Japan—one of the five Blue Zones (places where people live the longest)—create groups of friends who travel together and share the joys and pitfalls of life. They call these groups *moai*. Central to their success is their like-mindedness and respect and love for one another. Think of your communities as your moai. If the members aren't committed to the mission of the group or to you, in particular, you're better off without them. Positivity is a pivotal part of thriving.

Step 5: Get physical.

Can't you just hear the late, great Olivia Newton-John singing her hit '80s song? Like Newton-John, we're big believers in the power of getting physical. We've touted walking, resistance training, gardening, yoga, tai chi, and other physical movements in order to improve and maintain overall fitness and well-being. In this Hack's What You Can Do Tomorrow section, we cite love as an impactful way to thrive in your After-50s life. Getting physical in this way includes touching, hugging, kissing, and, yes, having sex. As we advance well past age fifty, it's natural for one's sex drive to diminish. The Mayo Clinic reports that many people enjoy sex into their eighties. The Clinic also says a healthy sex life is good for other parts of your life too—such as your physical health and self-esteem. Many studies show that sex releases a chemical compound in the brain called oxytocin, which increases emotional connection, elicits a sense of calm, and reduces the effects of stress. Add all this up and what do you get? People getting physical and thriving in life's Act II.

REMOVING OBSTACLES

Throughout this book, we've presented many obstacles that After-50s face in the quest for a long, healthy, joy-filled life. By now, you've learned how to face and overcome obstacles.

Here are a few about thriving, along with our strategies for hurdling them.

It's hard to identify a purpose at my age. This is one of the biggest challenges for After-50s, especially those a few decades past fifty. We're taught that career and family are what make people successful. Many After-50s are retired or empty nesters, or both. If one's career and child-rearing are over, they might think their purpose has ended. This is a depressing and debilitating attitude. In Step 2 of this Hack's Building Momentum section, we define purpose as what gets you out of bed each day. Remember, your purpose can seem insignificant to other people. You don't have to solve world hunger or cure cancer to have a purpose. And your purpose may be fluid; that is, it can change over the years or even over months or weeks. The simplest way to identify your purpose is to ask yourself why you get up in the morning. What do you want to accomplish? What brings you joy? What contribution are you making? The answer to any or all of these questions identifies your purpose.

I'm alone and don't have a community. We realize this is a big obstacle and a real problem. We also believe the solution is easy. Revisit your purpose, and find your community there. Do you love reading? Join a book club; you can find them at your local library, bookstore, or on social media. Do you enjoy wine? Join or start a wine club. Google "wine-tasting groups near me." Head to the tasting and find your community. We could provide more examples, but you get the idea. Like Okinawans, you're seeking like-minded people; you're looking for your moai.

I struggle with routine. It's a challenge to create good habits like eating right, staying hydrated, exercising, and getting regular, restorative sleep. We recommend integrating technology into your daily life. The tech can help you stick to your routine. Want to drink more water, take a morning walk, or do some deep breathing? As the saying goes, there's an app for that.

THE HACK IN ACTION

After battling various health problems in his fifties and early sixties, Don, a retired financial advisor, got serious about his health and well-being. He was overweight, suffered from Type 2 diabetes, and knew his situation had to change if he were to thrive in his remaining years. A father and grandfather, Don aspired to live many more years, and with both of his parents steaming toward their nineties, genetics appeared to be on his side. Still, health was a concern. He hired a physical trainer, lost forty pounds, and was soon pumping iron at a pace most competitive athletes would be proud of. He transformed his physical and emotional health in ways that would make anyone proud.

In 2017, an Ohio chapter of the YMCA, in a joint effort with the Cleveland Clinic, named Don the spokesperson for a new Type 2 diabetes campaign due to his remarkable journey to fitness at a time in life when most people would have quit. They filmed his amazing workouts and featured

Don's message in a film that has inspired thousands of people to change their approach to life with weight problems and debilitating diseases. Don was in the best physical and mental shape of his life, always smiling and eager to share his story.

Then came a global pandemic and, worse for Don, throat cancer. Years of work suddenly came crashing down. A seventy-year-old at the peak of physical fitness and overall well-being, and a symbol of health for all After-50s, he found himself fighting for his life at the worst possible time—when hospitals, medical practitioners, and most of his family and friends were in a different battle against a virus that kept them locked in their homes much of the time. Not only was Don in a fight for his life, but also the COVID-19 pandemic often made him feel like he was waging war on his own. "I went from the highest level to the lowest level," Don says. "I had a feeding tube; I couldn't eat, and I lost another forty pounds. I lost all of my muscle and fell into a dark hole. Every chemotherapy and radiation treatment left me weak and feeling sorry for myself."

Previously a symbol of the After-50s person this book is about, Don suddenly lost his Momentum Mindset. His strong body and mind and his joy-filled spirit disappeared. He was in a fight for his life, missing most of the qualities that helped him flourish in prior years. "I was a voracious reader up to the time I started radiation," Don says. "Then, I just stopped. I was too tired to read; I couldn't concentrate. Mentally, I was done. I had always prided myself on being well informed, up on everything. Read a novel every couple of weeks. Watched PBS. Studied history. As I neared the end of my treatment and entered throat therapy, I came to realize that cancer had been an inconvenience—not a death sentence. It hasn't changed who I am. Yes, cancer took away a year of my life, but that's all it did. I looked back on all that I had accomplished until cancer hit and realized that I had a do-over. I was still young. I still had a lot to do. I stopped the pity party. Once the feeding tube was removed, I forced myself to eat. I followed my therapist's instructions to the letter. I contacted my trainer and rejoined the YMCA. Now, I eat healthy, and I am slowly getting my muscle back. Cancer slowed my momentum. It did not stop it! My throat therapist now refers patients she fears are down mentally and not following her advice to me for encouragement. Her staff refers to me as an example of what a positive attitude can accomplish. I can think of no higher honor."

A true cancer success story, Don learned to thrive again when he revived his Momentum Mindset. Embracing his prior habits—feeding his body and mind and focusing on the positive—Don was once again hacking his After-50s life.

"I got back to good habits when I started throat therapy," he says. "Started doing things that stimulated my memory. I also started doing my hobbies again. I went back to restoring antique toys and slot cars. My mind got sharper, and my physical dexterity improved immensely. I also practically eliminated carbs from my diet, and I am mostly salt-free. No more fast food. In short, I got active. I'm out and about quite a bit now. My wife and I go out for lunch or dinner two or three times per week. We walk around stores to look at ideas for remodeling parts of the house. Activity! I cannot emphasize this more strongly. So far this year, I have seen every one of my specialists and they have all pronounced me healthy. I also curbed my temper. The guy who cut me off in traffic is in far worse shape than I am. Instead of yelling, I just shake my head and move on. I'm sure that there are things to vent about, but that's not one of them. I avoid controversy like the plague. Healthy mind equals healthy body. I also pray every night before I go to sleep. I've always been more scientific than religious, but prayer calms me at night, so I pray."

Most After-50s will run into one or more serious obstacles at some point. You may encounter an unforeseen tragedy, one or more deaths of family and friends, or a devastating affliction like cancer. These introduce physical and emotional turbulence, which makes it easy to quit. When you're hacking life after fifty, quitting is not a good option; thriving is. Don is our idea of a perfect example of thriving in life's Act II while using a Momentum Mindset. After beating Type 2 diabetes and becoming a symbol of After-50s health, Don faced a devastating set-back. He could have quit; he easily could have said, "This is the end." Instead, he stacked key habits—eating right, feeding his mind and soul, following doctors' instructions, and engaging with his community. He took charge of his life, deciding he had a lot left. Don continues to thrive. You can, too.

THE JOURNEY
CONTINUES

*This journey has always been about
reaching your own other shore no matter
what it is, and that dream continues.*
— DIANA NYAD, AUTHOR AND LONG-DISTANCE SWIMMER

I N 2022, WE were discussing overarching themes for this book. We'd been talking about health, fitness, longevity, and joy for many years, and the strategies we wanted to share were clear to us as we've been practicing them for a long time. We wondered, though, during one lengthy conversation, *What are some obvious, foundational concepts we hope readers would take away from this book?* As longtime educators, much of our thinking is grounded in what we've learned about people—both children and adults—during our combined sixty-plus years working in schools. We talked about communication, collaboration, performance, achievement, and growth. What makes people successful in these and other areas, we agreed, is that they constantly work to move forward. One of us used the word "momentum," and the other said, "That's it!" This is how we decided on the phrase Momentum Mindset.

As our discussions continued and, eventually, the writing began, we constantly talked about momentum and how it impacts After-50s and life's Act II. The ideas and strategies in this book do not work without momentum. In other words, you have to keep moving forward, and this doesn't always mean physical movement. After-50s movement is about forward motion in all areas of life—body, mind, and soul. When you commit to walking a few more steps, pushing or pulling a little more weight, reading a few more pages, talking to a stranger, taking more deep breaths, meditating a few minutes longer, spending extra time in nature, or planting one more flower in your garden, you build momentum. This momentum helps you thrive, and thriving is how to make the most of your After-50s life.

This book and our advice may end here. Our Act II journey, though, continues. Soon, we'll be well into the second decade of our After-50s lives, and we're not slowing down. Jim continues to teach, travel, write, love, laugh, and engage with his family and friends. When not writing, Mark is still building small businesses (he recently launched his second startup). He walks many miles daily, oftentimes with a family member by his side, and he and his wife, Mollie, are planning new adventures for when Mollie retires. This is just a little about us and our continuing journeys. We expect much more in our healthy, joy-filled, hopefully long lives as our battle with Father Time rages on. And we keep punching.

MEET THE AUTHORS

James Sturtevant lives in the suburbs of Columbus, Ohio. He's been semi-retired since 2019. He navigated thirty-four years in a public high school classroom. He now teaches future educators at Muskingum University.

James has been married to the stunning Penny Sturtevant for not only the entire twenty-first century but also the last portion of the twentieth. James has three children and two grandchildren. He's confident that more grandkids are on the horizon, and he wants to be around to meet them. He loved writing this book, and he *tries* to practice what he preaches. James is the author of five books that promote teacher well-being, bonding with kids, and student engagement.

Mark Barnes is a longtime educator, author, and entrepreneur. An avid reader and researcher, he became interested in—perhaps even a bit obsessive about—health, fitness, and longevity when he joined the After-50s club in 2014. Mark has written ten books, including *ROLE Reversal* (ASCD, 2013), *Assessment 3.0* (Corwin, 2015), *Hacking Education* (Times 10 Publications, 2015)—the first book in the internationally renowned Hack Learning Series—and *Hacking Life After 50* (Times 10 Publications, 2023)—the first book in the Hack Learning Life Series. Mark enjoys date nights with Mollie, binge-watching *Star Trek* with Ethan and Lauren, talking sports with his four closest friends, a.k.a. The Dudes, and listening to audiobooks. He also loves fantasy football and co-founded his league in 1990, making it one of the longest-standing fantasy football leagues in existence today … at least, according to Mark. Follow him on X (formerly known as Twitter) @markbarnes19.

ACKNOWLEDGMENTS

Jim

Special thanks to Penny Sturtevant for putting up with her extreme dabbling husband. She calls my dabbles jaunts. She always asks, "What jaunt are we going on now?" These jaunts can be culinary, fitness, spiritual, or intellectual. I'll confess, I've dragged her on some exotic ones. But she keeps up and often puts me to shame, like on our Rim to River to Rim hike at the Grand Canyon to celebrate her sixtieth birthday. Thanks for being a supportive partner!

Mark

Special thanks to these remarkable people. Stefani Roth, who listened patiently to my ideas about this book and offered her usual invaluable insight. Our amazing Times 10 Publications team—Jennifer Jas, Steve Plummer, and Regina Bell. Your expertise and professionalism are awe-inspiring. My good friend Jim Sturtevant. You're like a fine wine that only gets better with age. Penny Sturtevant for supporting Jim and me during this long process. All my siblings. Each of you has provided your own important example of living life After-50. My children, Ethan and Lauren. You make this journey a thrilling adventure. My wife, Mollie. Words can't do justice to the support, joy, and love you give every single day. I'm not worthy.

SNEAK PEEK

Next Up from the Hack Learning Life Series

HACK 4

MASTER THE MENTAL NOISE
Be a Good Friend to Yourself

*You cannot overestimate the unimportance
of practically everything.*
— JOHN C. MAXWELL, AUTHOR AND LEADERSHIP COACH

THE PROBLEM: OUR THOUGHTS
ARE OUR WORST ENEMIES

WHATEVER YOU ARE thinking about at a certain moment feels like the most important idea in the world. And then, as the thought fades, the importance of that idea fades as well, only to be brought back into shocking clarity when you think of it again. Our thoughts cycle around a few central topics most of the time. If we are honest, we admit that most of our thoughts swirl around ourselves, how we perceive ourselves, how we think others perceive us, or how we relate to a situation, object, or choice before us. By default, we become our most important thought, and our perception is shaped and colored by

231

the language of how we think about and talk to ourselves. Our thoughts of ourselves are a jumbled mess of anxieties and uncertainties, hopes and concerns.

Some might call it self-talk, self-esteem, or our internal dialogue. To me, it's just thinking. It is the way we process, the way we navigate a world too big for us to comprehend. The world is bigger than ever, and we are exposed to more of it daily. Not only are we exposed to a constant stream of ideas, but also, we are expected to make critical, rapid-fire judgment calls on how we relate to that broader world at every turn. And the infinite comparisons come next. Did I wear the right clothes, say the right words, and respond in the right ways compared to others around me? I don't look as good as them, feel as good as they must, sound as good as they do, or have the talent they have. The collision of our internal dialogue with the interruption of a big world creates an ever-present noise. Sometimes it is manageable; other times it is all we can hear.

If comparison is the thief of joy, then mental noise is the getaway car. Mental noise shows up as fear, reluctance, procrastination, insecurity, indecision, victimhood, or a complaining spirit. Nothing is more anxiety-inducing, fear-producing, or nagging than how we think about ourselves. We create narratives that we tell ourselves over and over. These help us navigate an insane world by creating shortcuts to understanding who we are and what we are about. I'm this or that, I'm this sign, I fit here, I don't fit there, I'm this type, I could never ..., and I will never ....

These stories serve a limited role and can hold us back from trying new activities, taking risks, seeing ourselves in a different light, or true self-reflection.

Most of the friction you face, the reluctance that hinders you from taking a needed step, originates and resides exclusively within your mind. If left unchecked, this mental noise can become your greatest obstacle and the most dangerous form of self-sabotage in your journey to sustainable health.

THE HACK: MASTER THE MENTAL NOISE

Mastering the mental noise begins with a recognition that how we think about ourselves has a tremendous impact on our trajectory. Perception doesn't shape reality, but it does shade reality. Imagine for a moment that you are self-conscious about a particular trait or feature you have. You walk around assuming everyone is immediately drawn to that certain thing and that it impacts how they relate to you. I could poll a hundred people who know you well, and the likelihood that anyone would mention that trait or feature is close to zero. Your internal perception is shaping how you show up, independent of what is happening outside of your thoughts.

I was always athletic and active, and I played multiple sports in high school and soccer in college. I was also very skinny. I struggled to eat enough and was underweight for my height, even well into my twenties. I remember visiting my grandfather and how he grabbed my ribs as he hugged me, joking that I was skin and bones. He was a kind man and meant well, but I was a young man, and that comment stuck in my head. I started to become more self-conscious about being thin and thought other people were looking at me through that lens as well. I don't share that story as if it were a traumatic event but more to illustrate an example of a mental thought pattern I had to work through.

Recognizing that much of your internal self-doubt does not match up with how others see you is a powerful tool. I continued to have self-doubt about my size and strength, particularly when I started working out at a gym. It took time for me to work through my insecurities about not being as big as other guys or not being able to lift much weight. In my case, I allowed how I thought about being weak to keep me from doing the activities that would get me strong. No one was watching. All of that was just in my head.

Here is the reality: You are the only person stopping you from being healthier. You can blame society, genetics, family history, your astrological sign, or your neighbor's dog that barks all night (okay, that one might be legitimate). But ultimately, you are an adult, and you are responsible for you. You make choices, you build habits, and you spend your money. And every choice you make, habit you build, and dollar you spend could be different if you wanted it to be. I'm not saying change is easy. But it can be *easier* if you recognize how you are getting in your own way. If change feels scary, good … it's supposed to. I love this line from Steven Pressfield: "Like self-doubt, fear is an indicator. Fear tells us what we have to do." The choice is yours: you can live in the safety of your labels and comfort zone, or you can expand past your current limitations.

WHAT YOU CAN DO TOMORROW

- **Filter out negative self-talk.** Your thoughts about yourself typically impact how you talk about yourself. Often, that shows up in the form of negative self-talk. One way to filter out negative self-talk is to change the person speaking and see how it makes you feel. What if the way you call yourself stupid after making a mistake was coming from your boss or advisor? How would that make you feel? Or what if the way you talk about your appearance was coming from your best friend? Would you continue to have a close relationship with that person if they persisted in demeaning you? You wouldn't put up with comments like that from your boss or friend, so you shouldn't put up with hearing yourself say those words, either. Your body is listening even if you don't realize it. Be a good friend to yourself, especially in how you talk to yourself.

- **Improve positive self-talk.** You can combat and improve your self-talk. Be aware of your inner dialogue. Are you conscious of it? What beliefs does your inner voice affirm about you? Does your inner voice ever affirm who you are or what you are doing? Reflect. Picture what it will feel like when you overcome your mental noise. Check in with yourself and put a check on the thoughts you let through your filter.

- **Confront your insecurities.** Give up the illusion of control, and stop waiting on the "right" time. Do what you can with the strength you have today. Set challenging goals by visualizing a big one that seems absurd right now. Focus on your strengths by leaning into what you are good at, and practice doing it better. Invite trusted, outside perspectives to weigh in. Listen to their input without internalizing it. Put structures and safeguards around your areas of weakness.

- **Ask three questions.** Author Jon Acuff wrote the book *Soundtracks* about the mental soundtracks that constantly play in the background of our minds. We might not hear them, but they influence us in some not-so-subtle ways. He talks about three questions we need to ask ourselves about our thoughts:

1. Is it true?
2. Is it helpful?
3. Is it kind?

If you answer no to any of these questions when you are stepping into an action or engaging in a thought, then it is time to reevaluate and change your decision or action. These questions have changed how I approach my thoughts and have helped me immensely as an individual, a dad, a spouse, and a business owner.

- **Ditch your labels.** It is interesting how we hate it when people label us, but we love to label ourselves. We tend to find safety in the labels we pick for ourselves. But those labels often hold us back from protecting our future in the way we need to. Ditch these three labels:

1. *I'm the type of person who* _____.
   You are more than your horoscope or your impulses. You can change. You can adapt. You're not done growing yet.
2. *I've always done* _____. You are more than your past. You can make new choices, take on new challenges, and create new habits.
3. *I could never do* _____. You are more than your fears. You can build courage. You can develop resilience. You can live fearlessly.

BUILDING MOMENTUM

When you've coached more than several hundred people, you start to see the patterns. You see the self-doubt, the old patterns they hold on to, and the fear of letting go of areas they have made part of their identity. You see the hesitancy to get on the scale, post progress photos, change their diet, or try a new exercise.

But you also start to see more inside the people you coach than they are aware of themselves. You can see an ability to push through what they doubt they can handle on those hard days. You see them grow into entirely new people with new habits, a new love for what their body can do, and new knowledge of how to care for it. It's a beautiful transformation to witness. Here is the takeaway: the new you exists just beyond what you don't think you can do, but you'll never be able to see it if you can't conquer your mental noise.

Step 1: Observe your version of "the man in the park."

You can't stop negative thoughts from popping up, but you can choose not to listen to them. Imagine you are walking in a park as the sun is going down. Few people are around, so you are startled when you hear a voice shouting in your direction. You look over and see a man gesturing wildly and yelling at you. As you get a bit closer, you realize he is both insulting you and demanding that you come closer. What will you do? You could go closer to him, or you could turn and find a different route through the park. We both know you'd find a new route. The hypercritical voice in your head is like the man in the park. Yet, we often choose to listen to him and put stock in what he has to say about us. The next time you hear that voice, remember the man in the park and actively choose a different route of thinking.

Step 2: Ask yourself, "So what?"

Take your biggest self-doubt, your greatest worry about what people are thinking about you. Sit with it for a minute or two and ask yourself, "So what?" I'm a people pleaser by nature. I want people to like me and think I'm great.

A fear of mine is that someone will dislike me, think my work is garbage, or express dissatisfaction with my performance. When I get caught up in that abstract fear, it helps me to ask, "So what?" So what if they don't like me or think I'm unintelligent? How will that impact my life in any real way? I quickly realize it won't impact me at all. Giving power over to these worries ties my self-worth to the opinions of others. By taking your worries to the limit of their logical conclusions, you can shift your perspective from the abstract to the concrete. Playing out the logical conclusions strips your self-doubts from having power over your choices.

DON'T MISS *HACKING SUSTAINABLE HEALTH*

AVAILABLE WINTER 2024 AT:
**Amazon.com
10Publications.com
and bookstores near you**

MORE FROM
TIMES 10 PUBLICATIONS

Hacking Parenthood
10 Mantras You Can Use Daily to Reduce the Stress of Parenting
Kimberley Moran

You throw out consequences willy-nilly. You're frustrated with the daily chaos. Enter parent mantras—invaluable anchors wrapped in tidy packages that offer cues to stop and reset. These will become your go-to tools to calm your mind, focus your parenting, and concentrate on what you want for your kids. Kimberley Moran is a parent and a teacher who works tirelessly to find best practices for simplifying parenting and maximizing parent-child communication with intention and without losing your cool.

Chasing Greatness
26.2 Ways Teaching Is Like Running a Marathon
Mike Roberts

Whether you are teaching a class or running a race (or both), *Chasing Greatness* is your roadmap to success. Teaching requires great endurance, and so does running. Both require dedication, sacrifice, and perseverance. After twenty years of teaching and more than fifty marathons, Mike Roberts is still chasing greatness. Now, he shares his experiences while showing teachers (and/or runners) how to run the most enriching race of your life and inspire your students and children along the way.

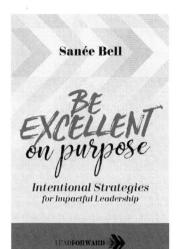

Be Excellent on Purpose
Intentional Strategies for
Impactful Leadership
Sanée Bell

Excellence is a journey where one discovers who they are, what they value, and the principles that drive them. But it's not always easy for educators to rise above the fray and live a purposeful life. To *Be Excellent on Purpose* means making a plan for life and working the plan to make it a reality. Teacher, author, presenter, and school leader Sanée Bell shares personal and professional stories and strategies that will make your leadership intentional and impactful.

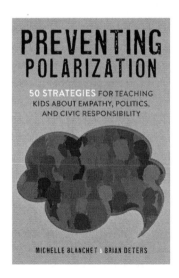

Preventing Polarization
50 Strategies for Teaching Kids About Empathy, Politics, and Civic Responsibility
Michelle Blanchet and Brian Deters

Break down conflict and build consensus. In an era that has become incredibly polarized, we can help our children learn how to come together despite differences. Michelle Blanchet and Brian Deters show how all educators can equip our youth with skills to become active and engaged citizens. A one-off course on civics is not enough. *Preventing Polarization* offers basic strategies that every teacher can use to create experiences to help students break down barriers through activities and role-playing. (Aimed at educators but a great read for all adults.)

RESOURCES FROM
TIMES 10 PUBLICATIONS
AND HACK LEARNING

10Publications.com

after50slife.com

Connect with us on social media:
@10Publications
@HackMyLearning
Times 10 Publications on Facebook
After 50s Life on Facebook
Times 10 Publications on LinkedIn

TIMES 10 PUBLICATIONS provides practical solutions that busy people can read today and use tomorrow. We bring you content from experienced researchers and practitioners, and we share it through books, podcasts, webinars, articles, events, and ongoing conversations on social media. Our books and materials help turn practice into action. Stay in touch with us at 10Publications.com and follow our updates @10Publications and #Times10News.

Printed in Poland
by Amazon Fulfillment
Poland Sp. z o.o., Wrocław
23 November 2023

44078517-ad08-4b7c-a9b2-a991b6aa787fR01